Tim,
Thank you for your interest
in this venture. I hope you
will accept this copy with
my complements.

Laura

*CHILDREN FIRST : Working with Children
and Disability.*

Laura Middleton

Published by
VENTURE PRESS
16 Kent Street
Birmingham
B5 6RD
Tel: 021 622 3911

First Published 1992

British Library Cataloguing in Publication Data

Middleton, Laura
Children First: Working with Children and
Disability
I. Title
362.4

ISBN 0 900 102 926 (paperback)

Printed and Bound in Great Britain by
Short Run Press Ltd., Exeter

To the Silent Valley

ACKNOWLEDGEMENTS

I have been more than lucky with the friends who have given up so much of their time to help with this book.

In particular, my thanks are due to Jo Campling, for the initial kickstart; to Margaret Kennedy for comments on the original concept; an anonymous manuscript assessor for candid and constructive criticism; and to Ann Gegg for sharing her considerable childcare expertise with me.

Ruth Eley waded through half-baked manuscripts on more than one occasion and, as well as offering her ideas, did a fine weeding job by eliminating hundreds of 'howevers' and 'of courses' which might otherwise have been left to litter my script.

Special thanks are due to Sheila Gough, not simply for typing the manuscript, but for her mysterious ability to remain enthusiastic about it.

Many disabled adults and children have helped shape my views and convince me of the need to promote the cause of disabled children as a social, rather than a medical, issue. I hope this book will assist in their struggle for equality.

All human beings are born free and equal in dignity and rights.

(Universal declaration of Human Rights, 1948, Article 1)

And the Lord spake unto Moses, saying, speak unto Aaron, saying, Whosoever he be of thy seed in their generation that hath any blemish, let him not approach to offer the bread of his god.

For whatsoever man he be that hath a blemish, he shall not approach: a blind man, or a lame, or he that hath a flat nose, or anything superfluous. Or a man that is broken footed, or broken handed. Or a crookbackt, or a dwarf, or he that hath a blemish in his eye, or be scurvy, or scabbed, or hath his stones broken.

(Leviticus, 21, v. 16 — 20)

CONTENTS

1. IMAGES

'Alas for Tiny Tim, he bore a tiny crutch, and had his limbs supported by an iron frame!'
(Charles Dickens, A Christmas Carol)

People behave differently toward a child who is known to be disabled. Over and above any handicap that may result from the disability itself, the child is faced with the handicap created by other people's attitudes toward someone who does not fit their criterion of 'all right'.

Such attitudes may not reflect deliberate unkindness. Indeed, they may be based on feelings of 'sympathy' for child and parents. But they do result in the child being marginalised as second best rather than treated as an equal.

The birth itself may be surrounded by a sense of tragedy; the parents may feel failures and attempt to protect their child from the harsher realities of life. They may strive to secure the best therapies in the world to restore their child to 'normality', neglecting other facets of personality and development in the process. They may apologise, hide their child away, and try to forget.

The rest of the world reacts by sympathising and raising charitable funds in a possible attempt to compensate for the fact that it will also mock, exclude and oppress.

In the midst of all the complex emotions and reactions centred on the disability, it is all too easy to forget about the child. This book is one attempt to redress the balance—to clear away the disablist clutter, if only by raising awareness of some of the processes, so that the child can re-emerge. The process of exclusion from society is described in Chapter 3, and other details of reactions to disability in Chapter 4. The second half of the book is then concerned with services and rights. Initially, however, these first two short chapters explore the background to our fears and

1

prejudices about disability by reminding us of the images, the humour, and the language which reflect and shape our attitudes as we grow up, and the roles we assign to disabled members of society.

Stories, old and new

Once upon a time, in the days of King Arthur, there was at Camelot a Great Round Table, with 150 seats for the best knights in the kingdom, each seat with a name on it. Only one seat remained unfilled at the height of Arthur's power, and that was the Perilous Seat, in which it was fatal for any man to sit, except for the Perfect Knight. One day, a youth came to Camelot who was so fair and perfectly formed that Lancelot dubbed him immediately, with the certain knowledge that his bodily perfection would be matched by his spiritual perfection. The young man sat, unharmed, in the Perilous Seat and later went on to find the Holy Grail. His name was Galahad. His perfect body was essential to his acceptance. If the knights at the Round Table had recognized someone with cerebral palsy as having the potential to be the Perfect Knight, things would be a lot different. We might note in passing that the perfect knight also had to be white, and young, and male, and uncorrupted by female company. Other heroes and villains fit the same pattern. Superman, modern American mythical hero, is not only able-bodied, his abilities and his senses are heightened. Only when he dons his spectacles does he disable himself, and become a weakling. Aragorn is born to be King of Middle-earth, and towers over his contemporaries both in physical prowess and in wisdom. By contrast, Gollum crawls on all fours, hides in dark corners and has a marked speech defect. Luke Skywalker is innocent, brave and handsome. Darth Vader covers his face and uses a voice synthesiser. The Daleks bear an uncanny resemblance to electric wheelchairs, while most of the other villains in Doctor Who are malformed humans. Pirates Long John Silver and Captain Hook had missing limbs. The Cyclops who terrorized Ulysses had only one eye.

The association of ugliness and badness is deeply ingrained: Caliban, the Ugly Sisters, Fagin, The Cyclops, hobgoblins, werewolves. Jekyll had to grow bent to become Mr. Hyde. Princesses, on the other hand, are young and slim with long blonde hair. Richard III, the wicked uncle, was a good deal less wicked before the Tudor propagandists decided to rewrite history and make him into the thorough-going rogue that suited their political purposes. Not only did they tamper with written documents, they also retouched his portraits so that Richard became the Hunchback. Deformed body equals evil mind. Everybody recognised it. The witch, too, is ugly as well as scary. We learn these things from childhood: firstly a standardised notion of what is beautiful, which will vary with the dominant culture, secondly to denote variations from this, such as physical impairment, as ugly, and thirdly that ugliness is bad. It is, therefore, not surprising that parents of Down's syndrome children have been tempted to alter the way their children look. They know our society is deeply influenced by external appearances.

There are few disabled children in literature, but Tiny Tim is classic.

> 'And how did little Tim behave?' asked Mrs. Cratchit. 'As good as gold' said Bob 'and better. Somehow he gets thoughtful sitting by himself so much, and thinks the strangest things you ever heard. He told me, coming home, that he hoped the people saw him in church, because he was a cripple, and it might be pleasant for them to remember upon Christmas Day, who made lame beggars walk and blind men see.'
>
> (Dickens, A Christmas Carol)

Disabled children are little and wise, suffer pain bravely and do not misbehave. And they never grow up. The nasty disabled adults mentioned earlier must have come from somewhere else.

Language

Language forms a barrier to understanding, something long recognised in the women's movement, which still strives to remove exclusive (chairman) and insulting language (little ladies).

The insult from such terms as 'spastic' and 'mongol' is fairly clear, as is the depersonalisation of language which refers to people as 'the handicapped'. On the latter, however, it is worth noting that the insult is not shared when the group so named is part of the successful, dominant section of society. I have yet to hear of a campaign to replace 'the rich' with 'people who have riches'.

3

Fears of able-bodied people about 'getting it wrong' are increased by the fact that language is a dynamic process, and what was considered all right a few years ago is no longer acceptable. Language alive today may well seem dated in a few years' time. The Curtis Committee in 1946 described a 'mongol idiot of gross appearance' and a 'three-year-old hydrocephalic idiot of very unsightly type'. (Curtis Report, 1946, para 140)

As recently as 1975, in a book entitled *A Constant Burden*, Margaret Voysey was able to refer to the 'normal family', discuss 'mental subnormality' and refer to 'mongols'. (Voysey 1975) The Penguin guide for parents of 'mentally handicapped children' still used the term in 1980. (Hannam, 1980) Happily, it has now fallen into disuse, although the equally offensive 'spastic' is still widely used. The 1989 Children Act used the term 'dumb' to refer to children without speech. Frequent changes in what is acceptable language occur as the stigma catches up. With old people we seem to have come the full circle. 'Old' was replaced by 'elderly'. The 'old people's home' became the 'elderly persons' hostel', without there necessarily being any other change. Soon it was 'senior citizens', a term now reserved for cheap tickets or hairdressing sessions. Then 'our elders' came from across the Atlantic before common sense, if not the residential units, reverted to using 'old people'. The aim has to be not simply to alter language to disguise a stigmatic condition, but to rid the condition itself of stigma and free it from oppression.

In the world of disabled people a similar debate rumbles on. From America comes the awkward 'differently abled', which betrays a liberal attitude and disguises the differences that lead to discrimination. 'Physically challenged' has been suggested, but I confess it conjures up nothing for me but knights on horseback. As I write, the current most useful terms are 'disabled people' and 'people with disabilities'. Martin Duffy, a broadcaster with disabilities, prefers 'people with disabilities'. (Observer Supplement, 2.9.90.) This means he is seen as a broadcaster first, disabled second. On the same page of the same paper Michael Oliver, a disabled sociologist, tells us that 'disabled people' is correct.

So what does it matter, and isn't it all just a debate about semantics? It does matter because people are oppressed by language. Disablist language patronises, offends and sets the tone by which we describe one another and set out our expectations. It is not simply the terms for disabled people that matter: it is the associated phrases that so readily trip off the tongue such as:

'MANAGING special needs', or

'COPING with disability' or

'BREAKING the news'.

'Do you SUFFER from a disability?' inserts an unnecessary negative value judgement into a common question. People are sometimes described in terms of their disability: 'He's an epileptic' or 'She's an asthmatic'.

Language both reflects and shapes attitudes. Our culture is based on beliefs which automatically stereotype forms of disability, in ways which are harmful to disabled people. In other words, we attribute additional characteristics to people whose bodies are not perfect. The most obvious is the assumption that people in wheelchairs are unable to make decisions for themselves: the 'Does he take sugar?' syndrome. America went to great lengths to ensure that President Roosevelt's wheelchair was not visible in photographs.

In 1981, Sutherland suggested that disabled people were at the same stage in their development as a homosexual is before he comes out. He suggested it was time for disabled people, especially those with hidden disabilities, to 'come out', and demand their civil rights. (Sutherland, 1981.) This includes the right to contribute as well as to receive: to pay for your round whether or not you need help drinking it.

Humour

Humour is a means by which people, especially children, learn their attitudes. I am not suggesting that disabled children have no sense of humour, but what sort of lesson is learned by the playground joke:

'What do you call a pile up of wheelchairs?'

'A vegetable rack'.

It is not just in the playground. A whole episode of the much-praised series Fawlty Towers hinged on the hearing impairment of one of the guests. The Mr. McGoo cartoon strip mocked his inability to see clearly. Stutters, too, are good for a laugh.

The disabled movement now has its own arts wing including disabled comedians, who use much of their performance time to raise disablist issues in a way that pokes fun as well as directs anger at the Establishment. Up to now, this remains primarily an internal consciousness-raising exercise, and has yet to penetrate to the breeding grounds of offensive humour. Sooner or later, however, a disabled comic will prove too funny for the mainstream to resist.

It is therefore possible to conceive of and practise alternatives. Some comedians have begun to acknowledge the fact that jokes can perpetuate oppression by stereotyping minority groups. Humour can be used to draw attention to disablist issues as well as to have fun at the expense of disabled people. Birkett's joke about the Daleks is one example (see below):

'Well, this certainly screws up our plan to conquer the Universe'

birkett

Reproduced by Permission of Punch

Images of Disability

Disabled people do not have to be the passive victims of so much modern television, awaiting charitable help. In a funny sort of way, the portrayal of disabled people as villains, such as Long John Silver or Darth Vader, at least gives them a more interesting character than the pale and grateful Tiny Tim. There are few images of disabled people as heroes saving the world, winning the war, or bringing about some notable social change. There are few media images of disabled people in roles where their disability is not part of the plot.

Disabled people are not usually portrayed outside special theatre groups as playing parts other than a disabled person. There are few parts for drivers, gossips, drunks, shopkeepers, burglars, con men, lawyers, teachers, politicians, drag artists, deserted wives, murderers, students . . . the fabric of media life. This gives us few role models of disabled people as being anything beyond being disabled, and allows blanket terms such as 'the disabled' to trip so easily from the tongue.

Even during a media event designed to raise awareness of the position of deaf people, the media managed to convey a second best image. During Deaf Awareness Week, 1990, much was made of the 'plight' of deaf people in their 'silent world'. The TV Times ran a two-page spread on the world of silence of deaf teenager Cathy Davies, who considers herself 'rather fortunate despite her deafness'. Cathy was described as 'bright eyed, clever, and attractive', a 'stunning, 19 year old with shoulder length ash blond hair and a figure any model would be proud of'.

'Sadly', the article went on, 'she cannot hear the wolf whistles she attracts'. Despite being an article about deaf awareness the next paragraph asserted that Cathy is 'trapped in a prison of silence in a world where noise is crucial to communication'. (TV Times 27.10.90.) Many able-bodied people have trouble accepting the reality of disability, and prefer images such as the contented blonde deaf girl. It helps them deal with their own distress at the thought of blindness if they believe that a blind person is somehow compensated by a heightened sense of hearing or extra-sensory perception. Blind people have been attributed with second sight, or the ability to prophesy.

Self Images

Disabled children constantly exposed to images that portray disabled people as second best, burdens or disappointments to their parents are bound to develop poor self images, and internalise the oppression. Too much emphasis on therapy to 'put things right' can have the same effect, where the growth of social skills is subjugated to the drive to make a child walk or talk at all costs. Children need to be valued for themselves, as well as given the opportunities to make the best of themselves. When too much emphasis is placed on one factor, such as walking, the price of failure is enormous because the child may believe herself to be permanently second best. Young disabled people with poor self images need to develop an alternative positive view. A negative view not only prevents them from having aspirations for themselves, it prevents them recognising the value of other disabled people as advisers, advocates or role models. Adult disabled people with poor self images are not born, but made. Disabled children need new images if the future is to be any different.

Social Work

Is there a role for social work in the image business? Social workers are in the business of changing attitudes and, daunting though it may be, an essential part of their task is to be sufficiently aware to challenge negative images. Disabled social workers may be in a better position to effect such changes: much depends on their own self image. Parents could be encouraged to take a pride in their child for themselves, not just for the achievements which take them nearer to an able-bodied image of the world. The child should receive praise for being who she is, and not made to feel less worthwhile because of an inability to do everything in the same way that another child can. Social workers with disabled children could make it their business to seek out and encourage positive images of disability. They could encourage others, and the child herself, to use positive language. They could foster the use of language which uses rights and entitlements, rather than terms like charity and need. Disabled children have a right to be here.

They could encourage the child to value her own body and appearance by not trying to hide or disguise it. Phrases like 'Isn't it a shame?' and 'What a pity!' should be discouraged, since they teach a child to despise herself or feel a failure.

Johnny Crescendo, a disabled singer, expresses his feelings against a system which tried to make him able bodied in a song 'I Love My Body'. It is an important thing for all disabled children to learn to do.

2. ROLES

All of us play roles: some are assigned for long periods, such as positions in families or jobs. Others are temporary, such as student or tourist. We intersperse the roles of shopper, passenger, claimant, client, complainant, changing 'our hats' accordingly. All roles carry certain expectations of behaviour and it makes life easier if people conform. There are even certain set lines in some set pieces.

'Can I help you?'

'Are you ready to order?'

These make the experiences of shopping, or eating out, familiar even in shops and restaurants not visited before. We know how to behave and what the rules are. Roles are parts which we learn. People stepping out of these set roles provide much material for comedians, but they also illustrate the tensions involved in staying within them. Basil Fawlty's strained smiles are an obvious example.

A disabled child also has an assigned role, or, more probably, a set of roles, in society. Moving out of these roles is disconcerting for people, and yet staying within them creates tensions.

One role for a disabled person is that of joker. The 'happy cripple', who constantly laughs off her impairment, is less of an embarrassment to the rest of society than the one who constantly demands attention, or rights. The disabled person who makes light of her disability, and never seeks to make anyone else feel uncomfortable, or obliged to move things around to accommodate her, is more welcome in social gatherings. It helps her to find acceptance. Margaret Morgan describes how hospital patients who are happy and make light of their illness are more popular with nurses. (Morgan 1975) It pays, therefore, to smile, even though it hurts. Fat people, stereotyped as jolly, may identify with this pressure.

Sympathy Role

The 'crippled child' attracts sympathy, and this can readily be converted into appeals for cash, particularly when she is brave and happy. In the nineteenth century abandoned children were deliberately mutilated by beggars to boost their takings.

Today the charity business is more sophisticated in its marketing and most of the dolls with callipers on their legs and collecting boxes in their hands have now been removed from the High Streets. However, it still relies on the same images of helpless reliance on the giver. The Spastics Society's first TV advert showed a woman in a powered wheelchair going to the shops, to the background accompaniment of coins falling into a can. The coins stopped, and so did she.

Such images are exploited to the full in the giant, fund-raising television events such as 'Telethon', where disabled children are paraded in front of the cameras to the strains of tear-jerking music. Disabled people, disgusted both by the images of disability and the publicity stunts of some of the stars, have protested and are receiving some media coverage, but it is clear the TV people are both puzzled and disappointed.

Many local papers find the story of local disabled children good copy provided they are suffering bravely, and seeking either an expensive cure or a piece of equipment appropriate for a disabled person. Some parents are more aware than others of the effects on their child of parading her as the grateful object of the town's charity, but there is great pressure if it is the only way to provide basic equipment where local authorities are themselves short of funds.

Charity makes the giver feel good. There is nothing intrinsically wrong with that so long as the object of the charity is not devalued by it. All too often charity degrades the recipient, so that the giver is not only seen as wealthier, but better.

Disabled children adopt the role of the handicapped—which derives from going cap-in-hand, or begging—because of the benefits which accrue from that behaviour, and because they are encouraged to behave in that manner by adult able-bodied people. Later the disability may be used to extract sympathy, or special treatment. People encourage and reinforce this, but only so far. Adult disabled people do not have the appeal of children, any more than adult stray dogs have the appeal of abandoned puppies.

Unfortunately, at the stage where disabled people realise they have reached a sympathy barrier, it may be very difficult to alter behaviour patterns.

Lifelong Child/Martyred Parent Roles

Another, not dissimilar, role occupied by a disabled person is that of lifelong child. It suits the lifestyle of some families that a child does not grow up, but remains a vessel into which care is poured. A severely disabled child is both non-threatening and permanently grateful. It is all too easy for a parent to slide into the martyr role, which substitutes for all other ambitions and rewards, bringing with it an entire lifestyle.

The lifestyle and meaning for the parent who is martyred revolve completely around the child, but it is the parent who is in control. To such a person, the more helpless and dependent the child is, the better. This is a distinct difference from a carer who is overwhelmed by the task and is trying her utmost to enhance the child's opportunities and abilities. The martyred parent can derive much satisfaction from the sympathy of neighbours and the blessings of the Church. Offers to help may be rejected, because solutions or improvements may not be what is really required, when medals and even sainthood are on offer.

The natural anxieties of such parents that someone else may cope better than them are exacerbated by a fear that someone may find the task easier, or make some improvements, and respite is usually out of the question. The role of the disabled child is therefore a vessel for caring, a burden, and a route to heaven. On earth, the martyred parent will arrange a lifestyle around the caring task. It brings visitors who would not otherwise bother. Harvest and other gifts arrive. Being looked after for by such a saintly parent, or foster carer, is not necessarily the best start in life for a disabled child. These are the children who can reach adulthood unstimulated and with additional physical disabilities because of lack of basic therapy. Neglected contractures in children with cerebral palsy can, for example, result in severely and permanently twisted arms and legs that may mean that even sitting in a normal position is impossible. This is preventable, but the idea that such neglect is a form of child abuse is a controversial one, which perhaps merits more of an airing.

Since 1970 all children have been entitled to education. This has meant that the care is, at least, shared and instances of children kept needlessly dependent should be increasingly rare.

Punishment Role

The other side of this coin may be the child who is viewed by the family as some sort of divine retribution: a punishment for sex before marriage or marrying without parental approval or an extra-marital sexual encounter.

This belief that disability is God's punishment for something is also held by some disabled people themselves, who regard their situation as retribution for some sin in a former life.

Both beliefs, based on guilt, lead to the same 'martyred' syndrome described above.

More justifiable guilt is visited on the parent who has really done something which may have affected the development of their child. Taking drugs or smoking during pregnancy can cause disability, as can a fall or an assault. Rejecting the offer of an abortion knowing that the risk of impairment is high can cause the parent to feel responsible.

The Scapegoat Role

A more complex role, found in a group or family where all is not well, is that of the scapegoat. The scapegoat gets the blame for failure or misfortune, and the group survives. So long as the real problems for the group exist, and are not tackled, the scapegoat is a necessary part of it. In a family with difficulties, who are likely to be 'known' to social services, a disabled child can easily become the scapegoat. It is important the social worker does not fall into the same trap.

Imagine a family whose father cannot budget properly, and whose income is low anyway, with a number of children who are in trouble at school. The gas is threatened with cut off with monotonous regularity, and the school is constantly demanding mother's presence to sort out one thing after another. Whose fault is it? The father's education? The system? The children? The school? It may seem that nothing much can be done about any of these: they are vast and overwhelming.

Add a child with asthma, or cerebral palsy, or epilepsy to the group and there is at least the possibility of putting all the family's ills into one basket. The existence of the sick or disabled child can now take the whole strain and the whole blame. Her needs provide a permanently available reason for every other member of the group to fail. There is the perfect excuse, the permanent 'if only', never to look for any solution or way out of multiple difficulties or failures to achieve. This pattern of functioning will find ready supporters among neighbours and friends. It will attract sympathy, rather than approbation, and will enable the downtrodden family to hold up their heads again. Poverty can bring shame: a child with disability can bring charity and hard cash, although probably never quite enough to enable a family to crawl out of the poverty trap. No one would suggest a family in poverty refuse cash, but the problem for families who function in the manner described above is that the pressures on them are to maintain the disability, because it provides benefits. The incentives to improve the lifestyle of disabled people are minimised by the system which operates on a SYMPATHY/CHARITY model, rather than a RIGHTS/ENTITLEMENT one. The prospects for the child with disability trapped in this culture are poor. This is scarcely the fault of the family already identified as one with problems in managing. They are only operating in the manner that society expects.

Professionals can also collude with the pattern of behaviour. They may talk about 'disabled families', and prolong the idea that the reason for the whole family's problems is the child with disability. As adults they will relate to the adult family members, accept their reasoning, and may well fail to try to understand the position from the point of view of the child.

As the pressures mount the child's asthma will assuredly get worse, not simply because stress plays a part, but because the family needs it too. Such families begin to need their disabled member in order to function at all, and a vicious circle of dependency arises. To remove the disability, either by cure, or alleviation, or the child into respite or permanent care, would not help the family because it would expose all of its real problems and difficulties.

Such families, needing the disability, resist such solutions with vigour, and can make social workers, or other outsiders concerned for the well-being of the child, feel powerless to help effectively.

There is a temptation to rush in and rescue, providing an alternative home where a foster family will nurture ability, and have no need for a scapegoat for their ills. It is not that straightforward. The crucial thing about roles is that, while the group may assign, the player accepts: sometimes having more choice in the matter than other times. The child with a disability in such a family has grown up with her role, and will probably play it elsewhere. The family, not understanding their own dynamics, will probably seek out another scapegoat or fail and break up. Removal is rarely the answer.

The child has accepted her role as the disabled member who disabled the family. She is unlikely to conceptualise this, as I have done, as the means by which her particular family functions. She is more likely, as she grows up, to feel guilty at having ruined everyone else's chances. Low self-esteem is common in disabled children and it is fuelled by a concentration on disability.

Unwinding such a situation will take time and understanding. Families have to come to value their disabled children for themselves, and not see them as a permanent handicap. This is particularly difficult because the family probably think they already do that. In their way, they are loving their child, and the chances are that none of the reactions they have encountered has done anything to challenge their behavioural patterns.

Clearly, the problems of the family need tackling in their own right. There is little to be done with the school career that has been disrupted, or the husband who, using the child with disabilities as a reason, gives up on his marriage. No social worker can be expected to heal it all.

Getting a family to take a pride in achievements, rather than exploit disabilities, is a reasonable, if time consuming, aim.

Scapegoating does not only occur in families. A nursery, school class or Brownie troupe can be equally guilty of blaming its problems on a disabled member. Again, the social worker may have an educative role.

Refocusing on the Child

What, then, is the alternative role for disabled children, if they are to cease to be society's means of feeling good about itself whilst condemning them to second class citizenship?

The answer is to return to the theme of this book, and state that the alternative to a disabled child being an object of charity, a vessel for caring or a scapegoat is to refocus on the child as a child first. The disability can then be relegated to simply a part of the child's experience.

Our society expects certain things for its children. This is not to suggest that these are always achieved, but we acknowledge something is amiss when they are not. The same criteria apply for disabled children. Children have the right to expect to grow up in a loving environment, to be protected from physical, sexual and emotional abuse and to be guarded against neglect. They have the right to enjoy play, and to learn about themselves and the world around them. As they grow they have the right to be taught to deal with the world: to take advantage of its opportunities, accept its challenges and cope with its threats. They have the right not to be exploited by others for financial, sexual or any other form of gain. They have the right as they grow to develop their own personalities and make their own choices.

Disablism

The politics of disability are not new. Louis Battye discussed the stigma of disability in a paper published in 1966, where he lists the societal roles of disabled people:

> '. . .an object of Christian Charity, a socio medical prob-
> lem, a stumbling nuisance, an embarrassment. . .' together
> with the function provided for others by his existence: 'a
> vocation for saints, livelihood for the manufacturers of
> wheelchairs, a target for busybodies'. . . 'but hardly ever
> taken seriously as a man' (Battye, 1966).

In 1981 Sutherland defined disabilities as restrictions imposed by society, and talked of discrimination. (Sutherland, 1981.) The theme has been developed by Michael Oliver, who has sought to define disability as a social, rather than an individual, phenomenon. (Oliver, 1983, 1990.) 'The Disabling Council' written by Allan Sutherland for the Local Government Training Board, takes a clear stance on equal opportunities and argues that the disability is the individual's own business, not that of their employer. (LG & TB,

1990.) The hub of the matter is that disabled people are not treated like everyone else. They are not socially accepted, nor fully integrated.

The powerful arguments put forward by the disability movement that disabled people are an oppressed group have resulted in calls for anti-discrimination legislation, such as exists to combat racism and sexism. There are, of course, parallels with movements of other oppressed groups such as the Women's Movement. Despite this, there is little evidence of a commonality of thinking, or an identity among groups of disabled people as part of an overall movement of oppressed people. Disabled men rightly complain of oppression because of their disability, but continue to oppress because of their gender. Neither the Women's Movement nor the anti-racism movement have really got to grips with the issues for disabled women or black disabled people, so there is still a tendency to imagine the disabled person as a young, white man in a wheelchair. There are few overall strategies to combat oppression. Indeed, the failure of one group of oppressed people to recognise their shared interests with other groups does much to undermine their effectiveness.

There is, perhaps, a tendency to dismiss disablist issues as non-contentious. Proposals to hold meetings in accessible rooms, loop systems, interpreters etc. may take a long time to reach agendas, not because of active opposition within the organisations so much as indifference. 'There's no point putting that on the agenda—everyone will agree to it.'

Disability movements emphasise the equality of disabled people as citizens; their right to work, to have a decent income and not to have to rely on charity. They emphasise that the person comes first, and that disability is a vehicle for their oppressions. They state that a person does not have to be able-bodied to have rights, or to participate fully in society. They object to television programmes that 'deal' with disability simply by restoring someone to able-bodiedness ('CONTACT' magazine of Liverpool Association for the Disabled, Summer 1990). Radical groups challenge the traditional Christian approach, where faith in Christ heals the crippled and restores them to full humanity and acceptability. (Linehan, 1990.) Jesus Christ did not appear to be able to cope with disability when he encountered it, insisting that cripples he met got up and walked. Yet he did not use his powers to eliminate it altogether. Change will only be lasting and real if it comes from disabled adults, children and their parents. Nevertheless, many disabled people believe their own bad press, and assist in their own powerlessness.

History teaches us time and time again that oppressed people take on the values of the dominant culture. In India during the days of the Empire, many Indians adopted white values and tried to be British. In the West Indies, black people straightened their hair and bought skin lighteners in a society where status rested on skin colour. Older people buy hair dyes and anti-wrinkle creams to look younger. Old people, as well as the dominant young, generally believe that old age means being unalert and non-productive. (Harris, 1975.) As long as people continue to believe that what they are is second best, their oppression will be made all the easier. All women are not feminists because many women actually believe that men know best. In the same way, many disabled people will deny their disabilities and try to pass as able-bodied.

The Greater London Association for Disabled People recognised this internalised oppression as a problem when undertaking their self-advocacy scheme for young physically disabled people, aimed at 16-to 21-year-olds. (GLAD, 1990.) They discovered that 'many of the young disabled people interviewed had no notion of their rights, the need to be able to make decisions or any levels of disability awareness'. (GLAD report, page 9.) They therefore felt it necessary to restrict participants to those having some exposure to the social model of disability, together with parents or teachers 'willing to allow' (!) the process of self-advocacy to develop. This recognition by the project leaders of awareness as a developing process points out a role for mediators such as social workers to act between those who overprotect and others who grow angry that all disabled people are not political animals joining them in their fight. The GLAD project encountered youngsters who disliked the aggressive stance of the disability movement, believing it jeopardised their partnership with the able-bodied world. They dropped out of the project rather than risk alienating teachers or peers by stirring up trouble.

This is not an experience solely of the disability movement. Women's rights activists will have experienced other women who refuse to recognise oppression, and will not risk causing trouble. Many black people are willing to believe they are fully accepted members of white society and do not wish to jeopardise existing relationships. At the root of all these opinions is a deeply ingrained belief that male/white/able-bodied is best, along with the values which that implies. Having internalised a belief that their race or gender or body is really second best, people are willing to settle for acceptance by, rather than equality with, the dominant group.

It is not enough, however, to believe that all is well because many disabled people do not themselves recognise that society discriminates, or that they are oppressed because of their disability.

While there is a clear role for active movements of disabled people, to campaign, offer support and raise consciousness, negative attitudes toward disabled people are a problem for the able-bodied, powerful sections of society to resolve.

Some groups have a greater chance of understanding the oppression of others because of their own experiences. Black people may be more receptive to arguments that disabled people are cheated of their civil rights. This is not always true for social workers, who see disabled people as dependent and black people as oppressed. A woman who is physically oppressed because she feels vulnerable walking alone should have some understanding of the vulnerability of a disabled person who cannot see or hear. This is not to suggest it is possible to share experiences, or that they are the same, merely an attempt to bridge the gap of understanding by identifying commonalities. A wheelchair user is oppressed and infantilised by both the height and sheer numbers of walking able-bodied people. Disabled children are right at the very bottom of the pecking order of oppression.

Effective social work with such an oppressed minority must first recognise the existence of segregationist thinking, which conceptualises one group of children as different from the majority.

Firstly, however, the following two chapters will deal with the process of becoming marginalised as a disabled child, and consequently oppressed as a disabled person.

3. SCREENING

Screening is the process by which the able-bodied world sorts out those who are different, and removes them from mainstream channels of life, for the greater good of the majority. It does this by closing down opportunities, and limiting people's visions. It works so effectively that many disabled people will come to blame their own personal shortcomings for their restricted life chances, instead of seeing the issue as one of a denial of civil rights.

In order to become a fully integrated, accepted member of society, with equal opportunities and responsibilities, a person must negotiate a number of hurdles. Failure to do so can result in the growth of a second class identity, low expectations, exclusion and discrimination. Screening is part of the process by which disabled people are identified, labelled, and marginalised.

From the beginning. . . . .

The first hurdle is the most dangerous: getting born. Failure to negotiate it will mean death by abortion, and you will not be consulted on the matter. The possibility that you may be a defective foetus is a ground for termination of pregnancy.

The second is being accepted by your family for who you are, instead of being punished for not meeting expectations, or being made to feel a burden.

The third is the medical screening by doctors and health visitors, looking for defects, by which you may be labelled.

The fourth is getting the right education.

The fifth is the perils of the market place, where items designed just for you are offered at special prices, and using ordinary living and leisure facilities.

The sixth is being allowed to grow up, experience the world, take risks and be a whole person.

The seventh is acquiring useful skills, being treated like an ordinary person, and fully exploring potential, rather than accepting that disability has predetermined limitations.

The eighth is getting a proper job, not being shunted into a sheltered workshop or training centre.

The ninth is finding your own place to live, somewhere you choose.

The tenth is acquiring a sense of belonging, and inclusion in the community as an individual in your own right.

The ten hurdles will be considered in more detail later.

Screening as a Concept

Screening should not be confused with surveying. A survey, usually for planning purposes, can be based on a sample of the population, from which the incidence of whatever is being sought can be calculated. There is no need to identify individuals.

Screening, however, aims to identify individuals. Any screening programme must investigate every one of a prescribed section of a population: all babies, all seven-year-olds', for example.

This can be intrusive, expensive and frightening. It is therefore pertinent to ask questions about the purpose and validity of screening programmes which have low accuracy rates, where the process is painful or uncomfortable or where there is no intended action as a result.

There is little advantage in screening for non-specifics like 'learning difficulties'. It is a vague concept with multiple causes, and many children will inevitably get labelled as borderline. Indeed, it can be a counter-productive exercise. Children so identified can easily begin to develop an image of themselves as failures, or not as good as other children. Young people who have been through the special education process have a marked tendency to defer to adult or able-bodied 'experts' even where it is their own life experience that is being discussed. Social workers undertaking school leaver assessments on the basis of trying to identify young people's aims and ambitions have found that a great many have not thought about it. They do not consider themselves as people with any potential, just people with disabilities to 'overcome'.

On the other hand, screening for a specific difficulty, such as reading, and providing extra help for the problem is a useful exercise provided the label of 'slow reader' can be avoided. There is always a risk of inducing feelings of 'not good enough' where children are measured against some concept of normality. The large numbers of children statemented as having special educational needs because of speech problems tells us as much about the expectations of 'normal' as it does about the children's levels of achievement. Lindsay points out the dangers of having registers that are simply too large to be of any practical purpose (Lindsay, 1984.)

In medical terms, useful screening is when the purpose is to identify specific, treatable conditions and the test is relatively accurate. Screening for PKU, for example, has provided a cheap test for the newborn infant for which a successful treatment is available to prevent the development of intellectual impairment. Less clear are the sets of pre-school developmental tests performed usually by health visitors. While the early identification of such conditions as hydrocephalus is undoubtedly a good thing, there is little clarity about the overall effectiveness of health visitor screening. Descriptive studies of the work exist, but there are few evaluative tests for the effectiveness of developmental screening, and they are usually critical. (Lindsay, 1984.) Health visitors are generic workers, advising on a wide range of subjects, expected to be experts on all ages and all conditions. They have large caseloads and visits do not usually last more than half an hour.

Concentration on weighing and measuring, on the other hand, can create much parental anxiety.

Surveillance programmes for children are only useful if the staff allocated the work have time, experience and the necessary skills. Attempts to screen children to predict the onset of disabling conditions have produced disappointing results, unlike those aimed at specific conditions, such as PKU. There is the risk of over-enthusiastic registration, and high numbers of children who later develop no difficulties are identified. (Lindsay, 1984.) False positive results nevertheless raise the spectre of problems and produce strong emotional reactions in parents. Even after their child is cleared many parents continue to feel uneasy and insecure. (Bodegard, Fyro and Larsson, 1983.) Parents themselves are as likely to spot something wrong as professionals, although they may not wish to believe it. Many parents who do admit to concern may find family doctors dismiss them as over-anxious. Freeman, Carbin and Boese report a Canadian study where over half the families' GPs refused to agree the children were deaf, and a third refused a referral to a specialist (Freeman, Carbin and Boese, 1981). Human development is not stable, and many children judged to have 'severe learning difficulties' or whose parents are told they will never walk/talk/work will later achieve 'miracles' attributed to many things, but usually explicable by the inaccuracy of the early predictions. Labelling someone a failure is dangerous and can be a self-fulfilling prophecy for children whose parents accept the medical prediction at face value. Predicting failure of children academically by the '11 plus' has long been discredited. There is no reason to suppose testing at any other age will produce better results. The controversy about the Government's imposition of Standard Assessment Tests for 7-year-olds and above reflects both parental and professional anxiety about the validity of such exercises.

Screening is never valid unless something helpful is offered to the individuals who test as positive. There is, nevertheless, a continual administrative pressure for children to be classified. Computerised registers require a series of codes by which children are classified. These can deny both the complexity and individuality of disability and are of no particular use to the children themselves. The danger of screening is that it can become less of an early intervention device for treatable conditions than an early-warning system so that children can be hived off from the mainstream. Various medical screening tests are available to pregnant women. None can guarantee a child without defects, but some offer a prediction of the possibility of disability. This will not usually indicate its severity. Tests, particularly the simpler ones, such as measuring the maternal blood level of alpha-feta-protein, can indicate foetal defects such as spina bifida, but a raised AFP level can also indicate twins. A false positive result, that is, one which looks as if it means a defect but turns out to be a false alarm, creates a great deal of anxiety for the mother.

Many women do not find the decision to terminate a pregnancy easy, for moral, cultural or religious reasons, even if they know of the possibility of a disabled child. The stress created for such women can, in itself, affect the pregnancy, especially if it causes the mother to increase alcohol consumption or take up smoking. Furthermore, the responsibility for the decision to bear the child is placed firmly with the parents. If the decision is made to continue with the pregnancy, and the child is born with severe disabilities, the emotional burden for the parents can be enormous. There is no one else to blame, and such parents are likely to decide that they have less right to demand help because they had accepted the responsibility knowingly.

The caring burden can be internalised and accepted, because the decision was made to 'risk' a disabled child. There is no release for anger or frustration by blaming poor medical facilities. This is bad enough for the parent, who has sacrificed the right to support, and who expects no sympathy, but it can be worse for the child who may be raised as mother's 'fault' and mother's 'burden'. Of course, it is not now possible to ignore the existence of the medical science that makes pre-natal predictions available. Most people want tests to reassure themselves the child is all right, although in practice no test is able to guarantee this. The process of testing can be lengthy in itself, particularly if the first stages test positive, and demand more detailed examinations. Given the complexity of emotions created during this process there should be a far greater availability of supportive counselling for parents with such dilemmas, for their sake and for the sake of their children.

The Ten Hurdles

1. *Getting Born.*
The probability of disability is a ground for abortion, and sympathetically viewed by most doctors. This whole issue is extremely difficult ground. On the one hand a woman should be able to exercise choice about whether or not she chooses to carry, and commit herself to caring for, a disabled child, particularly given the limited help she is likely to receive from society in raising her child. On the other hand, disability as a ground for terminating a pregnancy which would otherwise go to full term, reduces the status of disabled people to second rate. Cultures which expose female babies, or abort female foetuses carry the same message about the subordination of women.

Readers born with disabilities may have asked themselves the question, 'If my parents had known I would be blind/deaf/unable to walk, would I have been born?'

The effect is potentially devastating.

The measure of the taboo of disability in our society can be gauged by the fact that no similar questions are posed about people who are homicidal, or rapists, or sadistic. Such individuals do immense harm to the fabric of society and yet no funds are being devoted to the search for a means to identify them before they are born, to abort foetuses with a probability of turning out to be anti-social citizens.

2. *Getting Accepted For Who You Are.*
Knowledge that a child has a disability can cause a family to react in ways which it would not for a non-disabled child. This creates changed expectations and different behaviour. The disability can seem more important than the child. These processes are the subject of Chapter 4.

3. *Getting Medical Treatment.*
A further aspect of medical screening in early life is the equally difficult question of whether or not to treat children with severe disabilities. Bitter arguments can rage over such situations, where an assessment is made of a child's likely future quality of life. In October 1990 the case of 'Baby J' went to the High Court, where it was ruled that the child could be allowed to die should he fall ill:

> 'Without there being any question of deliberately ending the life or shortening it, I consider the court is entitled in the best interests of the child to say that deliberate steps should not be taken artificially to prolong its miserable lifespan.' (Guardian 20.10.90. Quoting Lord Justice Taylor.)

There is no doubt that this sort of case, where the child was born prematurely and probably would have not lived at all without prompt medical intervention, presents serious dilemmas. It is too facile to argue that medical science must always do everything it can to preserve life, with no thought for its quality. Equally, not carrying out life-saving procedures on some infants which would be available for others raises questions about the equality of citizenship.

A worrying factor is the degree of accuracy of medical science. The reports were couched in fairly indefinite terms: 'likely to be deaf,' and 'appears to be blind', whether he will be able to hold up his head is 'debatable'. Parents who have had the experience of being told their child will never do anything, or told to just take him home and love him, and later had a child grow up to walk and talk will retain a degree of scepticism about the validity of medical predictions so early in life. Later, disabled people can find it harder to get medical treatment when they are ill, because the illness is put down as being part of the disability. Conjunctivitis may go untreated if the person is blind. Children with cerebral palsy who have dislocated hips can find themselves the centre of controversy about whether there is any point in replacing them. Children with Down's Syndrome may be not considered worth a risky heart operation. Will the child with spina bifida get the first kidney available if she needs a transplant?

On the other hand, a disabled person may be regarded as someone with a permanent illness. There can be mistaken assumptions that it is catching: disabled children may be forbidden to play with able-bodied children in case it rubs off. There may be a search for a 'cure', with newspaper reports of trips to private clinics or to Lourdes. Even the term 'incurable' denotes a permanent state of ill health, not a difference in physical or mental ability.

4. Getting Educated.

The medical arena is not the only one in which disabled children may not have equality of opportunity. Educationally, there is also grave danger of discrimination. 'Special' is a term to be wary of in education, as it means not better but segregated. It is a sugary word designed to hide the fact that much education offered to disabled children is second rate. Once a label of 'disabled' is acquired it can be hard to shake off, and the majority of children allocated to special education tend to stay there. In many areas, 'special' nursery places are available earlier on the grounds of disability, or special needs. While the existence of the nursery may be a relief for parents, it can also channel the child into special education. Caring for the disability can easily become a substitute for educating a child.

An HMI report of 1983 concluded that a majority of the children who started out in nursery units continued their education in the same schools. Furthermore, if a child is assessed pre-five as having special needs, this compels the local education authority to make pre-school provision but reduces the rights to a place in mainstream school at five. The parents are excluded from rights under the Education Act, 1980, to express a preference for an ordinary school. Parents of rising fives with statements need great vigilance if they are to prevent their child from being sucked along the conveyor belt, simply because an early nursery place seemed a good idea at the time. Mainstream education is believed to function better without the additional difficulties placed on the teachers of unusual children. Standards in special schools are allowed to be different. Arguably, special education is aimed not so much at providing an education for disabled children, but at attempting to make them as near able-bodied as possible. Thus, medical interventions such as physiotherapy occur in teaching time, and are accorded priority. Great priority is given to teaching profoundly deaf children to communicate orally in English, and some schools actually ban the use of sign language as a valid means of communication.

The argument against special education has already been won at policy level, and integration is the aim of current legislation. It is nevertheless the case in practice that many children are still in segregated schools, and the arguments against them remain valid. Children in special schools are insulated from the real world: a feature which can be attractive to parents who are afraid for their children. Later in life, such children are less ready to enter mainstream society, and are in danger of living a permanent life apart. Many able-bodied children, on the other hand, grow up without meeting children who are different, and have to learn, as adults, the simple message that people with disabilities are people first. Experience in integrated settings indicates that children learn a great deal from each other, and that this works in both directions. The CSIE report on integrating Kirsty, a child with Down's Syndrome, found that school staff noticed the other children making her say things properly. (Centre for Studies on Integration in Education, 1983.) Had they had the opportunity to be educated alongside children with disabilities, employers who now display fear and prejudice at the prospect of a 'disabled worker' might behave in a less discriminatory fashion. Their discrimination is not based on malice so much as fear and ignorance: a belief that disabled people need looking after, and do not contribute to society.

This fear is a complex emotion, often based on how the able-bodied person feels they will 'cope', and reflects their needs rather than those of the disabled person. Distances involved in travelling to a special school are usually greater, and may be by special bus. This will probably either be bright yellow and appropriately labelled as special, or a very old smelly vehicle that should have seen the scrap heap years before. 'Yellow Perils' remain one of the more hated symbols of segregated schooling. Socially, children bussed to special schools miss out by not attending the same school as the other children in their street. Friends made in school will probably live at greater distances, a problem exacerbated by the added difficulties disabled children may have in travelling. Children are withdrawn from their natural environment and local community, to be placed with a group of children with a variety of conditions, who are equally isolated. In her report of pre-school education, Robson found that children with differing needs were placed together randomly, emphasising the use of special education as a dumping ground for those who don't fit the mainstream. (Robson, 1989.) Children who attend residential schools fare even worse, and the difficulty of maintaining friendships becomes acute. Many formative years can be spent away from home and family, with children whose own homes may be many miles apart. Only the children of the rich, who attend public boarding schools, share the experience, but with two main differences. After school, they will find it easier to maintain links through the easier mobility and communication available to the rich and able-bodied. More important is the knowledge that they are there because they are better than the rest. Rather the reverse is true for disabled children.

The curriculum in special education is more limited than in the mainstream. There is little incentive for teachers to push any but the brightest children, so if children do not work, the tendency is for them to be left to themselves and not be pushed. Vital areas of tedious, but necessary, education can be missed. 'My education was not structured or strict enough. My educators did not expect a lot from me.' (25-year-old with visual impairment and cerebral palsy.)

Time actually spent in school, as opposed to the bus, is shorter than in mainstream education, allowing less time to learn. There is an uncompetitive environment in which most children are not expected to succeed. Teachers who fail to make progress can always blame the disability, not question their teaching methods. By contrast, the sort of team teaching utilised in integrated settings, with helpers or interpreters, makes demands on the teachers to think hard about their teaching methods, and to plan lessons better in order to communicate with the rest of the team. This demands a higher calibre of teacher than a single individual content to amuse disabled children for the day.

Special schools concentrate on 'managing' disabilities, and in doing so fail to ascertain what children aspire to, and provide them with the knowledge and skills to pursue their goals.

Professionals who are trained to diagnose and treat disabilities run the risk of assessing the inability, not seeing the potential. Disabled children are more likely to have their visions talked out of them rather than have them encouraged, as if they had no right 'to have a go'. Even if children fail, there is satisfaction in trying, and finding out for oneself. Overall, it is a lesser regret than never even trying.

Children leave special schools with limited aspirations, and limited horizons. Many are pre-programmed for adult training centres, day care or a limited range of jobs suitable for 'handicapped people'.

Not only children in special education but also their parents, can feel intimidated and second rate. Kirsty's parents described a feeling of being kept in the dark over lots of things, because the education department, the professionals and the schools all made them feel they had more knowledge and information than they did. (CSIE, 1983.) Parents can gain confidence in an accepting educational setting. O'Grady reports that parents initially opposed to integration felt very positive after experiencing it in action. (O'Grady, 1990.) The move to place children in mainstream may not help, since many education departments will use a single, accessible mainstream school for all the disabled children, rather than adapting all their premises. The issues about bussing in terms of shortened days, separation from siblings and neighbours, and stigmatism still remain. Children may also be placed on trial at mainstream school, with the special school place ready in the wings should the child 'fail'. Kirsty's parents described this arrangement as being on tenterhooks. It highlights the difference in parental rights and security between parents of disabled children, and those of able-bodied children (CSIE, 1983). It is the school which should be on trial, not the child. In mainstream education, the focus of much discussion can be on 'managing the disability', rather than on how much educational progress the school is making.

Children are screened to exclude those who do not fit the 'normal' school criteria. Nowhere is this philosophy more apparent than in Hungary, where children who cannot walk do not go to school. The Peto Institute for 'motor impaired' children spends a great deal of effort in getting children to function in a way that makes them acceptable to the school system. The Institute has a long, forbidding flight of stairs up to its front door. The aim is to overcome handicap and become 'normal'.

If children fail to achieve the right to education by walking, their exclusion is their responsibility, not that of the society that built those highly symbolic steps. Allan Sutherland points out the confusion between illness and inaccessibility in the training video, 'The Disabling Council', with a story about a woman in a wheelchair unable to gain access to a building. Passers-by react by concluding she is ill, professionals by seeking a cure, and others by shipping her off to Lourdes. Sutherland comments that he has encountered many sorts of illnesses, producing rashes, boils and so on, but never one that builds steps. The conclusion, therefore, is not to treat the woman, but to build a ramp. (LGTB, 1990.)

Peto, in the form of conductive education, is coming to Britain. The ready acceptance of the Peto philosophy here is because most British people share it: people should be able-bodied to be a full part of society. It is unacceptable not to walk. Rather than offer the same standard of education to children who use wheelchairs, walking will be pursued at all costs.

Sometimes, the costs are quite high. These are not just in terms of air fares, or renting property abroad, but in terms of family strain where one parent is away. Brothers and sisters may be neglected as all attention focuses on trying to make the disabled child 'normal'. Bad walking can also cause physical harm. Children who walk awkwardly and at all costs are vulnerable to dislocated hips, and arthritis in later life. It can also cause pain. Good mobility in a wheelchair ought to be preferable for those children, but accepting bodies that can't walk for what they are is an alien concept and hard to get to grips with. It is important to listen to disabled people when they explain that they are happy in their bodies. It is wrong to assume that a person growing up with disability necessarily shares the attitude of an able-bodied adult who becomes disabled later in life.

Segregation continues into further education, where special needs courses are on offer at some local colleges. Colleges hold special courses in 'computer studies for the disabled', without apparently considering simply admitting disabled people to existing computer courses. The message of being second class is clearly transmitted through the current Youth Employment Training programme, where trainees with special needs are labelled as 'Category B'.

5. *Getting a Fair Deal.*

Outside the sphere of education, society seems to have learned the same lessons about marginalising disability in the market place. Disability provides a lucrative source of income for manufacturers of goods which people cannot do without. This would matter little if prices were realistic. People rarely protest when the need is embarrassing. In addition to high costs, it is not unusual to find marketing designed to work on people's guilt or social conscience.

Nottingham Rehab are currently marketing dolls 'brought in especially' from the USA which have disabilities but are depicted as active and sporty. They are designed not simply to give pleasure but to promote an understanding of disability. Nottingham Rehab offer to donate a percentage of the sales to children's charities. Who can resist, even though a small doll in a wheelchair costs £49.50. plus VAT? This is over twice the price one would expect to pay for a small doll. Children do not, in fact, need lots of expensive toys to play with, whatever the manufacturers would have us believe. Play is a means of learning, and can be achieved without any loss of enjoyment through the imaginative use of everyday objects just as well as through specially bought toys. Indeed, many specialist toys can restrict imagination because of their single function whereas a large cardboard box can be anything from a kennel, to a dolls' house, to a spaceship.

Not only toys but a whole range of leisure facilities are separate for disabled people. This is more than just the offensive exclusions that can occur when people in wheelchairs are not permitted into cinemas, pubs or clubs. It is the setting up of alternative facilities, principally day centres, where certain sections of the population are supposed to occupy themselves.

6. *Growing Up.*

After the hurdle of being allowed to enjoy the same leisure and play facilities, I mentioned the hurdle of being allowed to grow up. This is a complex situation, where children with disabilities are shielded from the realities of life by instinctively protective parents and teachers. It involves some risk-taking and some mistakes. It would usually involve some sexual activity. Young people denied these adventures miss out on the lessons that experience can bring, and learn only what others choose to teach. The result, which will be expanded on in Chapter 4, can be permanent childhood.

The final hurdles are dealt with more briefly, since they relate more to adults than children; but it is perhaps helpful to outline the full picture.

7. *Acquiring Useful Skills.*

The seventh hurdle identified was acquiring some USEFUL skills, as distinct from being patted on the head simply for turning up.

Courses for disabled students can be artificially 'easier' or operate according to different criteria. There is a mistaken tendency to protect, and to take on responsibility not for educating the student but for coping with the disability. The latter, as for a disabled worker, is the individual's own business.

Yet schools and colleges display remarkable reluctance to apply similar standards for disabled people on the assumption that they are aiding disabled people by making exceptions. Nice, kind teachers pass work that should fail, instead of seeking ways to help disabled children learn. This attitude only nurtures suspicions that the qualifications of disabled people are not worth so much. Giving people jobs or qualifications because of their disability is an extension of the same wrong thinking, and leads to real problems and resentments. They are seldom real jobs, and qualifications granted on such bases are rarely worth anything. They don't fool employers for long.

8. *Getting a Job*.

After acquiring useful skills, the next problem may be to find an employer who will give a person a job because of the skills, and work round the disability if necessary. All too common at present is the diversion of disabled people into sheltered workshops, where there is a limited career structure, and where the management are likely, in any case, to be able-bodied. Such workshops are typically in uncomfortable buildings, with a limited range of boring tasks, heavily subsidised by local authorities. Worst of all, disabled workers are kept out of sight, maintaining the cycle of fear and ignorance.

9. *Getting a Place to Live*.

After finding real work in an integrated setting, using real skills, the next hurdle is finding your own place to live. We are back to the issue of choice. There are housing schemes for disabled people, well built and maintained by housing associations. Another option is adapted housing within the mainstream community, with the risk of being isolated from other disabled people who may be more natural friends than the people next door. We cannot normally choose our neighbours. People will prefer different things. The usual situation at present is that only one possibility is available, on a 'take it or leave it' basis. Worse, particularly for people needing care, there may be no housing at all, forcing life in a residential unit as the only option to remaining in the family home.

10. *Acquiring a Sense of Belonging*.

Disabled people do not often have the option of belonging fully to society. In addition society likes them to be properly registered and labelled. Wheelchair users are conveniently identifiable. Blind people oblige with white sticks (symbol canes) and deaf blind people are encouraged to have a red-and-white stick. Perhaps the next step would be yellow for incontinent, or green for vegetarian. People who have epileptic fits are encouraged to wear bracelets saying so.

The denial of full citizenship to disabled people is further illustrated by their lack of voting opportunities. All too often polling stations are guarded by steep ramps, steps, heavy or narrow doors. Disabled people interviewed as part of a survey reported such things as voting outside polling stations or someone marking their papers for them. There was little knowledge of postal voting, which in any case is second best, since it involves making an earlier decision than the rest of the nation. More seriously, many disabled people had never registered to vote at all. (Fry, 1987.)

An Integrated Approach

An alternative approach to the present system of segregation into a second-rate world is necessary. This requires an acceptance that a disability is a part of a person, and not necessarily a part they would choose to change. Coping with it, if coping is necessary, is something for the disabled person and not for the teacher, supervisor or employer. Having cleared this attitudinal hurdle, the teachers, supervisors and employers will be left to concentrate their efforts on doing what they are qualified to do.

To take an example from social work, it is not uncommon for students with a disability to find themselves educating their able-bodied supervisor about their disability. Black students might find themselves in similar situations.

This spin-off of the placement may well benefit the supervisor, but it should not be confused with its purpose which is to enable the student to learn about social work. The supervisor of a disabled student can find themselves 'managing' the disability. or, worse, using the opportunity to deal with their own hang-ups about disability. While doing this, transmitting their social work skills - the main purpose of any placement supervision - can get forgotten. In the same way, able-bodied and disabled children have the same needs from teachers. Improvements to teaching methods, the use of smaller classes and the absence of environmental hazards benefits all children. To provide extra help in classrooms or better means of access to and mobility around buildings is not counter-productive, though it may be expensive.

Parents assessing the value of the education their child is receiving should be encouraged to ask questions about educational progress, not sucked into discussions solely about how the school is 'coping' with the disability, or how the child is 'managing'. 'How well are you doing in providing my child with an education?' is a more pertinent question than 'How is my child getting on?' Giving parents the self-esteem to stop apologising for their child and start making demands on educators to educate is a social work task.

Segregation is not the only option, however, as evidenced by the integration of profoundly deaf children by Leeds Local Education Authority. (O'Grady, 1990.) Leed's city-wide integration scheme covers the whole of the deaf community from birth to 16. Teachers and others were becoming disillusioned with the oralist philosophy which emphasises the acquisition of spoken English as the prime goal, and often bans the use of signing. Leeds worked on a policy which included both deaf children and others whose first language was not English. It was conceptualised as an equal opportunities philosophy by which the method of communication depended on the needs of the child. Children are given access to sign language and English, and to Punjabi as well. Hearing children have sign language classes also, and learn it unselfconsciously. Deaf adults are placed in schools as teachers, interpreters and helpers, to act as role models.

There are other models of integrated education which work well enough to explode the myth that integration is bad for the school system. Segregation is a matter of policy, and could be ended by its reversal. Linda Shaw reports on an integrated system from Canada, which is impressive in its philosophy of encouraging children and parents to have dreams. The planning process established shared visions, and sets about solving the 'stream of challenges' which arise in achieving that vision. (Shaw, 1990.) As well as dreams, the child's or parent's nightmares are examined: typically, ending up in an institution, or a sheltered workshop. Much the same fears are shared by British parents. Encouraging this 'looking ahead' allows fears and dreams to be dealt with. It is the opposite philosophy from that typified by the senior doctor who told Kirsty's parents 'Don't expect her to live very long: don't look too far into the future' (CSIE, 1983).

As part of the political process, disabled people will often prefer to organise as groups without able-bodied members, in the same way that women's groups are a useful source of support, awareness raising and confidence building. In the adult world the move toward equal opportunities is making painful progress, but it is probably fair to say that equal opportunities for disabled people lag behind those for other groups. An employer can no longer legally deny an applicant a job because of sex or race. No such legislation exists in this country for the protection of disabled applicants. Indeed, in its review of employment policy for disabled people, the Department of Employment specifically rejected the option of legal sanctions against discrimination, denying the rights of disabled people to such protection. (DOE, 1989.)

Underlying any changes is the need for a change of attitude which recognises the equality of all children, and in particular accepts them for who they are, not as second best because of some difference from the majority. This means acceptance that, for some children, sign language is their first language. For others, it means accepting that mobility is by wheelchair, not by walking. For children who use wheelchairs, this is not a second best, but their way of getting from one place to another. Putting up barriers to a group who use a different means of mobility is just as wrong as banning people on the grounds of a black skin. In other words, there is nothing wrong with not being able to walk. It is not a failure, it is a difference.

Further to this must be a recognition of the difference between being ill and being disabled. Appreciating that disability and illness are two different things is basic to adjusting attitudes away from the medical model that interprets disability as a kind of permanent complaint. Disabled people, like anyone else, can be fit or can be ill. The situation is further confused in some people's minds by the fact that severe chronic illness is legally defined as a disability: where a disabled person is someone '. . . substantially and permanently handicapped by illness. . .' (DHSS LAC 13/74).

The confusion is caused by false logic. While a chronic illness may well constitute a disability, a disability is not necessarily caused by a chronic illness. Coffee may be a drink, but a drink is not necessarily coffee.

The alternative to segregation is integration. We should be clear what we mean. Integration is not spending time in the same room as able-bodied children. A disabled child might be quite isolated in such a situation. Integration means belonging: having a right to be there, and being included. Integration is a philosophy based on equal opportunities and civil rights.

Segregation at present is compulsory, as the decision to segregate rests with the majority who exclude disabled people from schools, pubs or public buildings. This is not to deny disabled people, or any other group, the right to separate themselves for specific purposes. The issue, as always, is one of choice.

4. IN THE HOME

Children begin by loving their parents; after a time they judge them; rarely, if ever, do they forgive them.

(Oscar Wilde)

The Influence of Upbringing

A child is born with a set of possibilities: ignoring them may result in them never developing. No child is born a genius, only with the potential to become one given an appropriate environment. Disability should be regarded similarly. Children are born with certain inherited attributes, and may, uniquely, experience some trauma before, at or shortly after birth which gives them the additional characteristic of an impairment. Whether inherited or acquired, this is not a predetermining fixed characteristic, any more than any of the other potentials of the baby.

A label of Down's, no more than a label of cerebral palsy, or spina bifida, tells little. It does not determine intelligence, or life chances. It is impossible for anyone to answer a parent's frequent question about a disabled child,

'What will she be like when she is 21?'

and anyone who attempts to answer it with anything other than, 'I don't know' is scarcely to be trusted.

We can, however, confidently predict a number of common reactions to the knowledge that a child is disabled, which can profoundly influence their future quality of life: a sense of tragedy, fear, and protectiveness. These can lead to dependency, limited horizons, control, and oppression.

These reactions come from families and professionals, and are part of the process by which all sections of society systematically oppress and disable people who are different.

In order to break into this process of creating dependent, second class citizens, all of us will have to become more aware and more responsive.

In order to break into this process of creating dependent, second class citizens, all of us will have to become more aware and more responsive.

Children in Romania gave us a stark illustration of what can occur if potential is left undeveloped. The children discovered in the back wards of hospitals after the overthrow of the Ceaucescu regime were children disabled by their society in a particularly horrifying manner. They were underfed; had no sense of right or wrong; and no notion of how to play. Upbringing in the case of the Ceaucescu regime created children disabled by neglect in a Fascist dictatorship where there is an ethos of striving for racial perfection. Neglect is not peculiar to Romania, of course. Earlier this century, children in Britain were suffering similarly in large institutions. The 1946 Curtis Committee found instances of children confined to cots with dirty mattresses and clothing, no underwear, who ate from cracked enamel plates and fed and used their pots in the same room. The Committee found the children unstimulated and 'remarkably backward' because of their institutional lifestyles. (Curtis, 1946.)

This chapter considers various reactions to disability, and outlines the options as a child grows up and learns.

Reactions To Disability
1. A Sense of Tragedy

Knowledge that a baby has a disability is almost universally regarded as a tragedy, evoking sympathy. From that moment, parents lives are diverted from the planned path of 'normal' parenthood. In the American film *Kids Like These*, the experience is rather more optimistically described as like having planned a trip to Italy, having had all sorts of reports from friends who have enjoyed holidays there, and finding yourself in Holland instead. The guide books and advice are no use, and the process of exploration and discovery has to start from scratch, once the adjustment is made to being in another place. It doesn't mean it won't be fun.

Once friends know a child has a disability, the expected congratulations and celebrations turn into embarrassed silences and avoidances. People are not sure whether to send a welcome card to the new baby, or a sympathy one. Mum will probably be moved into a side ward, away from those whose babies are deemed normal. Dad doesn't feel like handing out the cigars, and if he does so, his mates will comment on how brave he is being.

Grandparents often find disability hard to accept, perhaps because they are not usually included in discussions with medical staff, or teachers. They may lack any experience of disability, and feel a sense of fear and lack of confidence in their role.

For the parents, it is a time of complex and mixed emotions. For the baby, however, there is no such tragedy. She has survived the trauma of birth, and is instinctively on the look-out for comfort and warmth and regular feeding. She is quite oblivious to the confusion and trauma she is causing. It is a simple point: often overlooked, but vital to understanding the lives of disabled children. To them, their birth, and their existence, is not a tragedy.

Social work has tended to respond to the parents in such situations by a form of loss counselling for the child they did not have. The theory is that parents will go through a period of mourning for the perfect, able-bodied child, and can be helped by counselling through the phases of shock, mourning and acceptance, until they pick up the pieces and proceed with life. Often parents are advised to have another baby as quickly as possible, and offered immediate genetic counselling to ascertain the probability of the next one being all right, or not.

The trouble with this approach, adopted from models of bereavement counselling, is that the child is still there and most parents will love and want it. Loss counselling reinforces feelings of rejection, confusing the disability with the child as a person, who has a need to be held, and loved, and accepted for herself. Loss is also a time-limited theory, the victims of which are supposed to proceed through a number of stages and then return to the normal tracks of life. A disabled child is a long-term project, taking at least as long to raise as an able-bodied child, and probably longer. Starting out on that path with the feeling that the child isn't really the right one is potentially highly destructive.

There never was another child, and there is therefore no one to grieve for. All parents may regret that their child wasn't cleverer, or better at football, or more musical, or seems unreasonably attached to My Little Pony. The child is not a second best, but a unique individual, to be raised as such and not damaged by constant comparison with something that she might have been.

This parental transfer of hopes and ambitions onto a child is, of course, not confined to children with disabilities, and neither is the adjustment and disappointment for parents as children break free or prove unequal to the tasks. However, the process of adjustment is collapsed when children are pronounced 'defective', and can seem to demand instant and radical rethinking. The danger is that parents in such states of shock veer completely to the opposite extreme, and entertain no ambitions for the child whatsoever.

Horizons and aspirations can change so that the child is only compared with others in her disabled peer group. Parents can easily fall into the trap of redefining what is 'normal' and measuring their child in terms of what is usual for children with that disability. The usualness of symptoms or behaviour is checked with medical or paramedical staff, so that the 'complaint' can be viewed as part of the disability instead of something new to worry about. While this may be understandable it is ultimately limiting, and produces false comparisons, since any disability manifests itself in a wide range of ways. Worse, it can disguise the fact that, while some conditions may be common, they are still subject to ameliorative therapy and require attention. If dribbling is ignored because lots of cerebral palsied children dribble, the result will be a dribbling adult, with obvious implications for social contacts and public acceptance, as well as causing unnecessary discomfort for the individual involved. Early intervention by a speech therapist may well be all that is needed to teach a child to swallow instead.

2. *Fear of Difference.*

Even parents experienced in raising children sometimes abandon all their skills in the mistaken belief that raising a child with disabilities is somehow fundamentally different. A new pattern of behaviour becomes established, and self-perpetuating, as tried and tested successful methods are suddenly thought not good enough. Not only parents, but relatives and friends' feel equally deskilled:

> when an able-bodied child is born into a family,
> relations and friends offer help and advice about
> problems and how to handle certain situations.
> When a disabled child is born into a family,

there isn't any offer of help or advice as people
don't know. (Sue Lane, 1990, Parent.)

It is important, right from the start, to see beyond the disability
to the child as a child. Controlling or preventing behaviourial
problems, for example, does not follow a separate set of guidelines:

do not answer unnecessary calls;

insist that the child sleeps in her own bed;

make sure time is allowed for all the family;

pay attention to, and reward, good behaviour.

Above all, avoid putting the child under unnecessary stress. Bad
behaviour results from anxiety, frustration, lack of control and
boredom.

It is not very easy to ignore a yelling child, but constantly rushing
to it reinforces the message that screaming long and loud will result
in being picked up, or given a bar of chocolate, or being allowed to
sleep with mum and dad. It is even harder to remember to reward
children when it suddenly goes quiet. Nevertheless, unless such a
pattern is established at an early age, the child will grow into an
adult with demanding behaviour that may not always bring a loving
parent in response.

Fear of difference leads to attempts by the able-bodied world to
make people fit into a pattern of 'normality', or risk exclusion.
Different means of communication, such as sign language, or
mobility, such as using a wheelchair, are regarded as second rate,
even though for many people they are the most efficient. Walking,
however badly, is praised. The purpose of walking should simply
be mobility, but it is also a passport to full membership of society.
The consequences for a child of reduced mobility because of a
reluctance to use alternative means are potentially very serious and
are detailed later in the chapter.

3. *Fear of Mistakes.*

Fear leads to over-caution, lack of confidence and an
over-reliance on professional help. Not only is this not always
available when required, it is frequently surrounded by the mystique
developed by people more conscious of retaining their own status
than genuinely helping. Parents can be frightened by the

responsibility of raising a child, and disability adds to existing levels of natural anxiety and caution. Fears of damaging their baby grow out of all proportion. Fear of making mistakes leads to an over reliance on expertise, whether from professionals or from handbooks.

Handbooks which offer brief guides to disabilities should be used with caution. Claims to provide details of the limitations which a disability imposes, for example, and to do so in a few pages, take account neither of the complexity of disability nor the individuality of the child, let alone the importance of her upbringing.

Fear stems from seeing the disability first, and ascribing too much to the 'medical problem' and expertise. In the video 'The Disabling Council', disabled contributors are critical of doctors who fail to validate their experience (LGTB, 1990.) Steven Liddle reports: 'I may not know exactly why my eyesight is like it is, but I think I know better than any specialist what it's like to see with my eyes.'

Professional status is part of a vicious circle not entirely the fault of the professional. Status is something accorded one person by another. Parents lacking confidence in themselves need the knowledge and skill of others, and practically demand professionals come up with answers. Honest answers such as 'I don't know' from a doctor may be interpreted as the doctor hiding something. Advice to treat the child like any other are dismissed as facile. Parents need the confidence to accept honest answers, not search for elusive expertise, and so restore the balance in favour of raising a child, not nurturing dependency.

4. *Protectiveness.*

Parents quite naturally want to protect their children, and this instinct is enhanced where the child is more vulnerable because of a disability. This instinct to protect, rather than equip for survival, can be counter-productive in the long run. Able-bodied children learn by taking risks and making mistakes. Parents limit the risk; give support throughout the failures and offer advice about better ways to deal with situations. Most young people, however, learn better by experience than through advice. No one pretends the process is not fraught with anxiety.

The world is unkind to disabled people who try to step outside the role ascribed to them. Parents recognise this instinctively, and try to shield their children from the worst of it. In doing so, they may deprive their child of the sort of pleasures described by disabled author Christy Brown about his own experiences of play in the streets of Dublin (Brown, 1954). The child is forbidden to play in the street. Brothers and sisters are admonished if they are too rough, or if they tease. This carries the additional spin-off of forming the attitudes of the siblings towards disability. The disabled child may be seen as spoilt, never punished, or given extra toys. Family outings revolve around them, and the able-bodied children may be expected to be carers.

Tom Wakefield relates one mother's view of her daughter's situation:

> 'Jacqueline made it very plain that although she never showed it to us externally, on the inside she was often quite resentful about the extra attention Andy had received. She even found that her own resentment of the situation made her feel guilty. . .'(WAKEFIELD, 1978).

Not all children will swallow their resentment, and there is some risk of physical abuse while parents' backs are turned.

In offering the shield to the disabled child parents may not only fail to be aware of ALL their children's needs, but may also deprive the disabled one of the steady bombardment of knocks and disappointments which enable her to develop a protective shield of her own. If children do not learn to cope, a real tragedy will occur when the parental shield is no longer there. The child may be in their fifties by then, with none of the skills or knowledge to survive outside an institution, or to exercise any choices at all. Raising this spectre with young parents may not be a pleasant way to spend the afternoon, but it is a realistic and necessary exercise. Most parents do think with dread about the future, and are receptive to such discussion, even though the reassurance they want, that there is somewhere just like home waiting, may not be available.

Some parents spend years trying to find more safe walls to shield their children, bouncing from disappointment to disappointment. This is a soul-destroying journey, which cannot ever have a happy ending, because no one will ever care as much as they do. Institutions may be safe, but they are not like home: mum and dad aren't there. To escape this trauma children have to be allowed to grow up.

5. *Control.*

Protectiveness, which is a natural reaction, all too easily develops into control, such as deciding where and with whom the child plays.

Such control persists into adulthood and can be stifling.

Such children develop no mechanisms for coping with life except by evoking sympathy because they are disabled. No one explains that disabled adults do not rate the same degree of 'oh, what a shame!' as children do. Making a decision as an adult, expressing an opinion, or describing an ambition will prove impossibly difficult. The disabled person, even when addressed directly, will turn to a parent or parental substitute for assistance. This is not just about major life decisions, about which most of us will consult, but on trivial day-to-day matters, such as the clothes to wear, or the filling of a sandwich.

Parents do not control and smother children because they are trying to produce dependent and nervous adults. They become locked into a process which may be based on natural protectiveness, but does not allow nor encourage growth and development because of an ingrained societal belief that disabled children should be treated differently, as if in need of continual protection. The urge to keep 'safe' continues into adulthood. Society controls disabled people because it tries to prevent them ever growing up.

6. *Oppression.*

The anti-racism movement has long recognised the importance of teaching a child not only the mechanisms to deal with discrimination, but to be proud of who they are. It is worthwhile for parents of disabled children to consider a similar approach, instead of raising a child to strive constantly to achieve or copy an unattainable 'normality'.

Many parents of disabled children are, of course, able-bodied, and will never have the personal experience to draw on. Criticisms of parents are a feature of writings by adults who have grown up with disabilities (e.g. Sutherland, 1981.):

> even the most accepting and supportive of parents are,
> if they are able-bodied, unlikely to be able to avoid
> contributing to one aspect of our oppression, which is
> our lack of cultural identity (p.101).

This creates, through no one's fault, an immediate disadvantage for the child, as she lacks a parental role model. Able-bodied parents have a very real problem in trying to equip their disabled child with the skills necessary to survive the hostilities of a discriminating society, let alone to have the confidence to explore their ambitions and 'go for it'. The tendency therefore is to strive to make them able-bodied.

Policy on fostering black children with culturally matched foster parents recognises, among other things, that they have the personal experience to understand the implications of being black in a white society. No one, of course, would seriously suggest removing disabled children from their natural parents to provide the kind of experienced parenting that is impossible for able-bodied parents. However, there has yet to be serious discussion about appropriate foster or adoptive parents for disabled children, and whether disabled parents should be actively recruited. Indeed the opposite is more probably the case. The stage of development in thinking about the needs of disabled children reflects an unproven assumption that able-bodied people are better parents.

Where natural parents are disabled themselves, this can also present some disadvantages. There may be an increased sense of guilt if an hereditary condition is passed to children. Even if parents are free of this themselves, other members of society are likely to be judgemental in their attitudes. It is popularly held that people should not knowingly bring disabled children into the world: this is one of the roots of oppression.

In some situations, being raised in a disabled household can create social isolation. Deaf parents and children, in particular, face difficulties in the local community because of the language barrier. Unlike other linguistic minorities, deaf people do not tend to live in communities, and have to travel over much wider areas for social contacts. This is easier if money isn't an issue, or if people are not tied by young children.

GROWING UP: Healthy and Unhealthy Learning.

Most disabled children are raised within able-bodied families. Far from preparing them for life in an integrated society, this can shelter them from learning the mechanisms with which to cope with discrimination, or even with the everyday rough and tumble of survival in the outside world.

1. *Developing an Identity.*

Disability is a social concept. In the same way that the child has no concept of her birth as a tragedy, she has no in-built disabled identity. If this develops, it will be because it is learned from the attitudes of others. This can start from a baby sensing the parents' disappointment and grow as a negative feeling about herself as socially inferior. Instead of growing up being a time of increased self-confidence and widening awareness, it can be the experience of learning about prejudice and inequality. This can translate into reduced life chances and low expectations.

The aim of raising children should be to equip them with positive self images, so that disadvantage occurring as a result of the disability is placed rightly where it belongs: in the discriminatory treatment received from others, just as it would if they were black, or discovered they were gay. People do tend to exclude, or to mock, or to prevent exploration or risk taking. If the child is treated differently from her brothers and sisters on the grounds of her disability, she will acquire a negative self image as she grows.

Children can learn to use their disability as a means of gaining attention, or goodies, rather than using their own personalities. They become interested in their own disability instead of showing a sociable interest in others. Nancy Finnie emphasises the importance of teaching a child, however disabled, to help others, in order to develop a likable personality and social competence

(Finnie 1974). The first stage is developing an awareness of the needs and wishes of others, rather than seeing them simply as people who are there to offer service or to neglect.

Children who can get out of the house to play not only develop a better sense of spatial awareness, but also learn social skills, reciprocal behaviour and to conform to the norms of peer groups: to belong. Children who are unpopular are those who are socially retiring, do not share, and are uninterested in others. An immobile child is therefore deprived of the opportunity to develop awareness of the social skills which operate in a group. Parental fears that they may be hurt, either physically or by teasing, can keep them from letting their child out with the others, even if this means thinking out ways of doing this safely. It is only by mixing with other children that the child will learn what is accepted behaviour, what gets laughs, and what will cause rejection. The disability in itself will be merely a source of curiosity to a group of young children, not a stigma. That is for older people who have learned its meaning. Learning to get on with others is much more sensible than attempting to hide because of a disability, which may, in any case, only be a difference. Unlike parents, a group of children will not make the child the centre of the universe, and so will assist her social learning and aid her success and survival.

Social interaction is about learning the rules of social behaviour, which vary by class and by culture. Children do not learn by constant exclusion. Those who know the rules have the higher status.

Adults with disabilities are rarely accorded the same dignities, nor given the same responsibilities as able-bodied adults. People are less likely to argue with them, get angry, or even to address them directly. Disabled people may be sent free drinks, or not allowed to buy a round, even when they have the money to pay. This may seem nice for a while, but it is essentially being treated as second class.

In allowing others to provide all the time, you are not only denying yourself the right to decide what is on the menu, you are also losing status and dignity. You are not equal.

If it comes at all, realisation of all the missed experiential learning will come with anger.

Social work with disabled children is too often informed by work with disabled adults, particularly those disabled since childhood, rather than by child care principles. This approach can miss the importance of childhood as a life stage in itself, not simply a preparation for adulthood. While adults who develop disabilities are in the best position to know what that feels like, and to recognise the discrimination they face, they are not in the same position as children born with disabilities, who have never experienced being able-bodied, hearing or seeing. They have no comparison to make, nor any need to reassess identity, cope with loss, manage a change in status or family situation, or adjust personal attitudes to disability.

A disabled child learns more slowly about the prejudices and inequalities of the world, with the result that growing up, instead of being a time of increasing self-confidence and widening awareness, can turn into a negative experience of increasing realisation of rejection and limiting horizons.

In no groups is the difference in lifestyle and culture more marked than between those born deaf and those who lose their hearing after language is acquired, most usually in old age. The latter group do not identify with deaf culture, belong to the deaf community nor use its language. Nevertheless the services for the two groups are often put together administratively and in terms of service delivery.

Deaf children are not in the same situation as adults who have lost their hearing, despite the 'medical' similarity in their condition, that is, the inability to hear.

Neither is the child who has never walked in the same situation as an adult who loses that ability, or a child who has never had vision in the same situation as an adult adjusting to loss of sight.

I propose to explore more fully the situation of one of these, the child who cannot walk, to illustrate the differences of the pattern of development from a walking child.

2. *Growing up with limited mobility.*

Inability to walk means a permanent differential of height, where others not only move, but are literally looked up to. This in itself can create feelings of inferior status, as the disabled child fails to keep up with walking children of the same age, or younger. The child may be unable to distinguish between things of different heights—tall and short are difficult concepts for a child who is permanently on the floor or sitting.

If children later do stand, objects such as furniture often prove to be much smaller than they had supposed. (Finnie, 1974, p.241.)

Unlike an able-bodied child, the child who cannot walk misses the sense of growing up and growing taller. Only the immediate carers may actually know how tall a child is, and many parents talk of the length, rather than the height, of their non-walking child, however old.

Growing in height means a changing relationship with the world, which implies more status and more control, not to mention the ability to get at things that were previously out of reach.

Being permanently at a low level can restrict views too. It may be impossible to see out of the window for example. Sadly, lowering the height of windows has not been accorded the same priority as accessing toilets or lowering light switches.

Riding can offer a solution to being permanently down there. Horses are best, but dad's shoulders may be a decent substitute, while the child is light enough. This offers a much better view than the cradle-hold often adopted for disabled children, long after they have ceased to be babies. Being on a horse brings a different perspective on the world, and a feeling of superiority and confidence that goes with increased height. It can also be fun.

Not walking means not only lack of height, but also lack of mobility. This has more-far-reaching implications than an inability to get independently from place to place.

Babies learn about movement by waving their arms and legs about, and finding out what happens. A child who is mobile finds her own way about the house, opening cupboards and drawers and exploring the contents.

By running herself or her toys into things she learns what will move and what is solid and needs to be gone around. By losing things she learns what is meant by under, and over, behind and in front, and so to move up and down and around. If a ball rolls away she learns how far to go to get it back, and how long it takes. Later this will translate to judging distances, and calculating speeds.

Children therefore acquire a sense of space, from moving around in it. A child who cannot crawl will miss out on this independent exploration unless some other form of mobility is substituted.

Lack of mobility also means a child cannot move to toys or things of interest, nor away from danger. The former restricts opportunities for the child's self-motivated stimulation while the latter increases vulnerability. Child abuse will be dealt with in a later chapter, but even relatively harmless things like family pets, or irritating aunts, have to be borne since they cannot be avoided.

To counter the inability to move, a child may develop other means of control. In this respect, there are similarities with the behaviour of an immobilised adult lying in bed ringing a bell for attention. The young child may be less conscious of establishing control, but that is what is occurring. If it works, however, it may be at the expense of being respected and liked for one's own personality, since people respond to the disability not the person.

In some ways, it is less a matter of establishing control than retaining and developing the mechanisms of babyhood: crying, screaming, throwing things, refusing to eat, being sick. The immobility of the child reduces her options. Physical contact, such as tugging at a skirt, or climbing on a knee, are not possibilities. Even eye contact may be difficult. Screaming and crying therefore retain their position as the principal means of attracting attention.

A child can seem like a spider at the centre of a web, managing information and people in so far as they come to her. Later, she may be a disabled adult, confined to an adapted bungalow, managing her world in the same way: from a fixed spot, with services and people coming, or not coming, to her. It is a different view of the world, with disability at the centre.

Social proximity may also be a problem if a child has a poor sense of spatial awareness. Social competence depends on developing a sense of proximity appropriate to the situation and the other people, as well as correct orientation and posture.

Wheelchair users have a more limited range of non-verbal signals. They do not have access to the range of sitting postures usually available: upright to attention, leaning forward earnestly, slouching nonchalantly, relaxed with crossed legs or feet on the table. Positions involving standing up are impossible. More effort is therefore necessary with facial and verbal expression.

A single wheelchair user in a group of standing people, at a party or conference for example, can disrupt people's patterns of interaction, since they either have to talk down or sit down themselves, losing contact with the main group. It is necessary to start to operate in an extra dimension.

The occasion is made all the harder if the wheelchair user is immobile, or has no sense of spatial awareness, so that he unwittingly intrudes. Some disabled people hold court in such situations, but they can equally well be ignored or patronised, or get the dubious benefit of being a captive audience for someone's monologue. Independent mobility, combined with some social skills, is infinitely preferable. The rest is up to the walkers to develop skills of their own which include operating on different levels.

Developing independent mobility will aid the acquisition of spatial awareness, and lead to the development of social skills. A child who can decide for herself where to go and when, within the same limits as an able-bodied child of the same age, can choose to fetch her own toys, turn on the television, or answer the telephone. Mobility aids should be considered as soon as possible, even if the child has the chance of walking.

Able-bodied children ride push bikes or toy cars before they can walk, but there is a great fear that providing disabled children with mobility aids will somehow sap them of the will to walk.

A similar and equally false argument is made against teaching deaf children to sign, in case it prevents them from talking.

Children can ride bikes, and swim, as well as walk. Mobility in all forms has its own rewards, and learning by one means that it is good to get about encourages a child to try other things. An electric wheelchair, even for a young child, can open up the world and allow the child some choice and control. Bikes or pedal cars are options if the child has sufficient leg power. The first bikes, or sit on dogs or trains, are pushed along by feet on the floor. Failing this, a lower aid may be moved with the hands.

3. *Towards Independence.*
The process by which parents are persuaded to allow their disabled children to enter the adult world—maybe to have a place of their own—is usually referred to as 'letting go'. Conceptually,

it implies a single event, which is potentially traumatic. There is, of course, a moment in many people's lives which can be identified as a symbolic moment of independence, or gaining adult status: leaving home; reaching 18; going to college, getting a front door key, but ideally becoming independent should be a process, not a single event.

Preparation for independence from parents should be a gradual growing process throughout childhood. It starts by leaving the total dependence of the womb and breathing independently; through feeding independently and so on. Children learn the consequences of their actions and gradually take on responsibilities. Such things as choosing and buying clothes do not need to wait until a person leaves home. A teenager's room can become their own responsibility. Getting a key is a milestone: a symbol of trustworthiness.

Yet this gradual growth of the feathers necessary to fly the nest is all too often underdeveloped when a child has a disability. Adolescence, in particular, is a time for self and sexual exploration, misbehaviour and rebellion: out of which trauma, sooner or later, should emerge a young adult, ready for independence from the family. This metamorphosis is signalled to the world by the donning of different clothes, hairstyle, make up and language; and the adoption of different heroes and heroines. Each generation has its own views about what is suitably outrageous: it is all part of the natural process of breaking free.

Disabled adolescents frequently miss out on this whole growing experience. They are shielded from sex, often with the kindest of motives, to protect them from the disappointment of not being able to find a satisfactory relationship. Their clothes are chosen by their parents; their hairstyles are conventional. Nothing distinguishes disabled young people faster from their age group than old-fashioned clothes and haircuts.

Rebellion in the form of walking out, slamming a door, staying out late, pinching sweets, sagging off school or buying a motor-bike are all avenues which may be denied a young person with limited mobility, or who lacks the ability to communicate orally. Frustration may find other routes and lead to behaviourial problems, which, as likely as not, will be attributed to the disability.

Leaving home may be delayed many years until it is forced by the inability of parents to care any longer; so that the disabled person then requires what are variously termed 'rehabilitation' or 'independence training programmes'. Independence training is part of growing up, and should be on every parental and educational agenda. Even if the young person continues to live in the parental home, it is wise to maximise their responsibilities and their choices within the setting.

Since independence has become a fashionable buzz-word, it is important to be clear what independence means. It does not mean isolation or having to manage alone. It certainly does not mean having to spend four or five hours getting up and dressed, and becoming thoroughly exhausted by the process, if you would prefer to use a helper to get you up in ten minutes and spend the morning doing something more interesting. It does not mean spending hour after hour in a rehabilitation centre learning to peel potatoes, make scones, wash dishes or iron clothes when none of these skills are essential to a rewarding lifestyle.

Independence means having control, making decisions about one's own life, and exercising choices, thereby retaining self-respect and dignity.

The alternative means parents enabling their child to obtain as much control over her life as possible, and involves exposing her to experiences as she grows, such as is done with an able-bodied child. Some risks have to be taken, so that later decisions and choices are based on actual knowledge and experience.

Social Work

This chapter may have seemed hard on parents, who are portrayed as lacking confidence, taking control, not allowing their children to grow up, and treating them in a different way to their other children. It is therefore important to remember that this behaviour reflects the values of society. The chances of social work intervention changing anything may seem remote, but facing huge hurdles and challenging societal values are not anything particularly strange to social work. They may not, however, be usually associated with social workers 'with the disabled'.

This is therefore, the time to explode another myth. If it is to be effective, social work with disabled children and their families is not an easy option. It demands the best of social work skills. It is a matter of grave concern that some departments relegate it to their lowest priority, and allocate the work to inexperienced, unqualified and least-competent staff.

However, it can happen that an otherwise good social worker reacts like an otherwise good parent facing disability, particularly a disabled child, for the first time. She can panic.

I suspect fear of disability to be the reason, and such comments made to me over the last few years as 'I don't know how you can work with children like that', have been frequent enough to confirm my suspicion. That social workers share the fears and prejudices of the rest of society about disability is not surprising given the low profile of many disabled people, and the lack of attention to disability awareness on training courses until the last few years.

Few social workers would dream of making such a remark in relation to black people, being conscious of the racist nature of such thinking, yet a residue of revulsion remains for people who are in some way impaired.

Confidence disappears for social workers as it does for parents, because the same socialising pressures exist for them. The disability is thought to be beyond their expertise. They lack all the answers parents are bound to want, and which seem to be expected from them. They have been cast into a role of expert which they do not feel. All their skills and knowledge suddenly desert them.

Like parents, social workers become reliant on professional expertise, usually medical. They scurry to look up the disability, and suppose that this little knowledge will see them through. They respond to the parents, demands for information about the disability which they are ill-equipped to offer, and forget about their skills in child care, in family work, in groups, in emotional counselling. They offer to send an occupational therapist, a nurse or a welfare rights officer. And then they disappear for 15 years.

If there is one single message that needs to be transmitted loud and clear it is that many social workers already possess all the skills and knowledge they need to support and work with a child with a disability. It is simply a matter of their being awakened to that knowledge. Social workers of the future do not require specialist training about disability: they require a sound set of social work skills, together with an awareness of disability as an equal opportunities issue.

What knowledge is necessary? Beyond valuing the rights of individual children, and the energy to try to change their situation alongside them and their parents, clearly some information is necessary, not to enhance professional status, but to share and to use. A knowledge of the benefit system, and other sources of financial help, can help take the sting of poverty out of a situation. For children unlikely to achieve financial independence in adulthood, some knowledge of setting up trust funds is useful, although a list of solicitors who are clued up is more helpful. Avoiding giving the family's hard-earned savings over to the DSS or local authority should the individual require long term care is the main pitfall. A knowledge of the legal rights of the child is important: or at least where to go for help. Knowledge of local support groups and facilities, such as groups for parents or disabled people, allows people the option to seek peer group support. Useful skills will be those of advocacy, or the ability to help a person become their own advocate. Assertion, communication and organisational skills are basic to good social work practice.

Social workers need knowledge of child development and family relationships, and should be consciously engaging this expertise from the outset: seeing beyond the disability. An understanding of family dynamics helps in a family with a disabled child, just as in any other. Many disabled people are able to recall being spoilt as children, allowed to get away with things, and given extra treats. This is not a recipe for developing into a caring, sharing adult who will make friends because they have concern for others and do not expect the world to revolve around them. Intervening to 'nudge the wheel' is a skilled task, as the problems may not be seen as such by the family since they lie in the future. Parents coping with day-to-day demands can find it difficult to envisage how life might be in a year, or in 20 years.

Relieving immediate stresses is a prerequisite for tackling the longer term objectives. This involves a range of more immediate skills.

Oliver highlights three areas: providing emotional support, providing access to practical assistance, and reducing the negative impact that dealing with an unfeeling bureaucracy may have. (Oliver, 1983.)

An ability to negotiate on behalf of an individual is essential to secure the best possible deal from other agencies, such as the Education Department or the DSS. Knowledge of basic welfare rights is essential, although the field is a specialism in its own right in some areas.

These will all relate in the first instance to the parents and older children, since the baby has no immediate need of direct social work help. It is too easy to remain as the parent's social worker, particularly for an able-bodied worker with able-bodied parents, but conscious efforts have to be made to represent the child.

This involves ensuring that parents and others look beyond the disability. As the child grows it means relating to her as a unique individual, not assessing her against a list of strengths and weaknesses. Constantly asking about how a child is managing this or that, rather than finding out what she enjoys and trying to share that, will reduce the child's status in her own eyes.

Much can be learned from young children in the relationship game. Free of social prejudices, they accept differences at face value, ask questions simply out of curiosity, and deal much more fairly with people than adults and older children who have learned about the pecking order. Parents could be encouraged to deal honestly in return. Any other response creates a mystery, and a taboo. Disability should not need to be hidden.

Forming an honest and equal relationship with a child is, therefore, a vital task, if representation is to be truly representative. Relating to a child need not be at the expense of relating to parents if such a role is adopted when she is young and becomes established practice.

Social workers need to develop skills in communicating with young children and to do so in the way they feel most comfortable. There is a range of methods available, and children are less self-conscious and more flexible than most adults. Singing, drawing, playing with dolls, dressing up and play-acting are all possibilities far more appealing to children than sitting talking.

With older children and young adults parents respond very differently to the social worker who addresses the child directly. It is one fairly speedy way of working out who in the family is in control. Parents who are encouraging growth and independence in their children welcome it. Others intervene immediately and there is rarely much help from a young person trapped in this way. Parents have to be tackled directly about the control they are exercising and their reasons for perpetuating the childhood of their son or daughter. This requires much patience and understanding. Where it has become very hard, I have sometimes resorted to using a second worker for the parents, so the child has her own social worker for a while. This can help break the mould: social work students make excellent partners in such a plan.

Accepting a child for who she is, beyond the disabled label, is basic to any effective social work intervention. With a baby, it may be important to demonstrate this acceptance to the parents, in order to begin to deal with any feelings of shame or rejection. This means reacting to the baby as if you were not aware of an impairment. There is no precise formula, since social workers and children vary, but the repertoire includes talking, holding, admiring, playing, and getting down on the floor. Later it means listening, watching and more playing. Taking an interest in what interests the child, rather than concentrating on discussing disability, is not only an important step in establishing a relationship, but is one of the building bricks, for the child, of a positive self image. This is not to suggest that the impairment should be ignored. It is, after all, probably why the social worker is involved in the first place. A sense of proportion should be retained, however. Social workers can be tempted into adopting the wrong role and pressed for their medical expertise. It can be all too easy to give it, in which case the real issues are left unexplored and contact with the family remains at a superficial level. In these circumstances the social worker is just the nice person who pops around for a chat and translates what the doctor said into plain language. Social workers become medical go-betweens, rather than concentrating on social needs. The position of a hospital-based social worker, trapped between a forceful consultant and a confused parent, is not an easy one. Nevertheless, it is important not to lose sight of the child in all the talk of her disability.

Social work therefore requires not only an awareness of child development, but also what particular restrictions can be caused by some disabilities, or social response to them. It is not simply the child's inability to walk or talk that creates all the difficulties described earlier, but the failure to recognise the importance of mobility and communication, by whatever means are most efficient.

Social work also involves soaking up the emotional responses of the child and their parents to their situation. It is important that social workers learn not to attempt to invalidate the emotion. Children need to cry and to get angry if they experience pain, frustration and injustice. Telling someone they have a right to feel angry if they are cheated is more helpful than trying to calm them down because you cannot cope with the intensity of feeling. Allowing people to cry when they are in pain, or in trouble, or feel life is hopeless is more helpful than trying to get them to stop because the worker is embarrassed or uncomfortable. Adults usually apologise for their tears, and it helps if the social worker says its OK to cry.

Afterwards, directing the feelings into some useful action may be appropriate, and help to prevent the growth of gnawing bitterness that is born of feeling powerless and exploited. More simply, directing anger elsewhere helps prevent ulcers and stress, and may even effect some change. It can be important, however, that anger is not directed in its original form, but is used to fuel strength of purpose and a reason to persist.

While therapeutic for the child or parent, soaking up anger, pain and frustration is emotionally draining for the social worker. They need to understand their own capacity to do this. The adrenalin produced during crisis work (traditionally, but in my view wrongly, regarded as the most stressful branch of social work) is not there to help. Sitting for hours and soaking up distress, some of which may have been bottled up for years, is emotionally very draining. It is hard work—which is why many workers latch on to the first practical thing they can think of to do or to provide, however trivial, to justify their visit.

It is unusual to see 'reason for visit—listening' in a case file.

Listening is tiring, and workloads should reflect this. This is a lesson for management, which will be dealt with in Chapter 6.

5. THE LAW

The Children Act 1989 introduced a new legal category of children in need, which specifically included disabled children. New obligations were laid on local authorities to register and to provide services for this group. For the first time, disabled children were specifically included in children's legislation, integrated with other groups of children, rather than being included, almost by default, in legislation designed with adults in mind. Apart from two other Acts: 1970 Chronically Sick and Disabled Persons Act and the 1986 Disabled Persons (Services, Consultation and Representation) Act, previous welfare legislation ceased to relate to children. The change in legislation reflected a healthy change in philosophy which saw disabled children as being children first, disabled second, acknowledging that all children had common needs and placing a duty on local authorities to provide packages of services to compensate for the disabilities.

The other major relevant legislation affecting disabled children is the 1981 Education Act. Again, the underlying ethos is one of integration. Social work staff should be wary of assuming the Education Act is something only for schools. It is vital to the quality of life for children that they receive the best possible education. The Act is concerned with children's rights, and involves parents in much debate and negotiation with local education authorities. The support and representation of a social worker or other advocate can be vital in ensuring that local education authorities do not bulldoze parental wishes to suit the needs of the authority. In some cases, someone will have to take on the responsibility merely for explaining the Act to parents, who may not always realise the significance for their child of the bits of paper which drop through their doors.

As far as local authorities are concerned, law is either mandatory or permissive. It places a duty on local authorities to offer certain services, and permits them to offer others. The priorities usually set by local authorities are based firstly on legal 'musts', followed, if budgets permit, by legal 'mays'. As far as children with disabilities are concerned, the tendency has been for the service to be part of the 'may' category. Even with the advent of clear mandates under the 1986 Disabled Persons Act, many local authorities have failed to respond, relying possibly on the Government's own lack of enthusiasm to fund what started as a Private Member's Bill.

The following is an account of the terms of the major legislation of concern to disabled children. It is organised on the basis of the order in which disabled children are likely to be affected by legislation, rather than the dates any particular piece reached the statute-book.

The Children Act 1989

The Children Act simplified the law relating to disabled children by restricting the scope of local authority functions under the 1948 National Assistance Act and the 1977 NHS Act to adults, retaining only the definition of disabled from the 1948 Act. In section 17 (11) of the Act, it defines disabled children as follows:

> A child is disabled if he is blind, deaf or dumb or suffers from mental disorder of any kind or is substantially and permanently handicapped by illness, injury or congenital deformity or such other disability as may be prescribed

Mental disorder is defined by the Mental Health Act as 'mental illness or incomplete development of mind, psychopathic disorder and any other disorder or disability of mind' (Mental Health Act 1983, Section 1).

This, therefore, includes children affected by 'physical disability, chronic sickness, mental disability, sensory handicap, communication difficulties and mental illness'. (Guidance to Children Act.)

The Act places a clear duty on local authorities to keep a register of children with disabilities. Hopefully, such registers are drawn up in conjunction with local health and education authorities. The idea of registers is to assist in service planning and registration and should never be a precondition for service provision. As with adults under the National Assistance Act, the criterion for service provision is 'registrable' not 'registered'. Registration is voluntary on the part of parents and children, and local authorities would be quite wrong to apply pressure to register. If parents and children can recognise the advantages in a register, there will rarely be a problem. All too often, sadly, maintaining a register becomes an administrative end in itself.

More important than the Register, the Act places a duty on local authorities to provide services to minimise the effects of disability, giving disabled children the opportunities to lead lives 'as normal as possible' (Schedule 2, Para. 5.) This is, of course, open to interpretation, but local authorities committed to improving services are given an open brief. They are not restricted by the shopping list of services provided for in the Chronically Sick and Disabled Persons Act (1970). The overall development needs of the child should be considered in a full assessment which includes not simply an MOT-style functional assessment centred on the child, but an examination of the environmental barriers and difficulties which impinge upon her. The Act allows for this legally and encourages it philosophically. It moves thinking away from the typical medical or deficit model into a social or ecological approach. It remains a major task for parents and professionals to ensure that action is taken, and disabled children are not simply palmed off with the occasional piece of hardware. The Children Act gives local authorities the power to arrange assessments of any disabled children, which can include health or education services. In the past, all these authorities have tended to do independent assessments. The Act encourages a more collaborative approach, and the co-ordination of services. (Schedule 2, para. 3.) The primary objective is to safeguard and promote the child's welfare. This is not necessarily achieved by direct services to the child, but requires some lateral thinking. The Act talks of family support services, not specifically children's services. The local authority is asked to put together a package of services which could include services to the home, such as home helps, or services elsewhere, such as a day nursery. The latter does not necessarily have to be for the disabled child but could be provided for a sibling.

The Children Act therefore allows for a detailed assessment and an imaginative use of resources. It requires local authorities to commit themselves to provision in this area. Unlike the Education Act and the Disabled Persons Act it is not constrained by detailed procedures. It is vital that parents, professionals and organisations of disabled people work together to ensure that the possibilities inherent in the Act are realised, so that, 20 years on, it is not necessary to overlay it with time-consuming and bureaucratic procedures.

The Education Acts 1981 and 1988

Since the Education Act of 1971 abolished the category of 'ineducable', all children have been entitled to an education, up to the age of 19 if required. The 1981 Education Act went further in encouraging integrated education, although the number of escape clauses included has ensured the continuation of segregation in practice, particularly for children with learning disabilities. Parents seeking a mainstream education for their child still often have to fight for it. There are three hurdles to get across before a local education authority can be forced to integrate.

1. Integration must be compatible with the child receiving the special education he or she needs.

2. The other children in the school must continue to receive an efficient education.

3. There must be an efficient use of resources.

Not surprisingly, the definition of terms such as efficient is left to the local education authority. Any one of the above is enough to provide a determined head teacher with the reason to exclude a disabled child but it is important that such attitudes are challenged. There is nothing in the above which should justify exclusion because of inconvenient steps or inaccessible toilets, both of which are solvable practical problems.

The Act outlines a complicated 'statementing' process, in which parents (or local authorities having parental rights) have the right to comment. There are set times laid down for parental comment at each stage of the procedure, although the local education authority can take as long as it likes. Parents can be penalised for failing to produce their child for assessment pertinent to the Act, although there are no penalties on local education authorities who fail to keep their part of the bargain.

The right to comment, and be consulted, has tended to favour the more articulate parents. Many keep sophisticated files on their children, and it is advisable for a social worker to encourage all parents to adopt this practice, keeping a record of all communications from the local education authority, and a copy of any letters sent back. Education departments can be daunting and there are clear advantages in having an advocate, such as a social worker, involved in the process. The process, as it should happen, is detailed below. Suggestions for dealing with the Education Department are made in Chapter 6.

Stage One:
Either the local education authority proposes to carry out a formal assessment to discover a child's special educational needs, and tells parents by letter,
   or
parents request a formal assessment which the local education authority cannot refuse, unless the request is 'unreasonable'.

Stage Two:
Local education authority gives written information to parents explaining the assessment process and their rights during it, plus the name of a local education authority officer to go to for advice and information.
Parents have 29 days to send in comments on the proposal to assess, either by letter or by interview with a local education authority officer.

Stage Three. . .after 29 days.
Either the local education authority decides to go ahead with the formal assessment, and informs parents by letter of its decision and the reasons for it,
   or
the local education authority decides not to go ahead, and informs parents by letter. It does not have to give reasons in this case.
Parents who disagree with the local education authority's decision can appeal to the Secretary of State for Education if they believe the local education authority is acting 'unreasonably'.

Stage Four:

The Assessment. The local education authority collects reports from school, educational psychologists, medical staff, parents, possibly social services.

Some reports will be based on examinations of the child, which the parent can usually attend and to which they can submit information if they wish about their child, including any independent expert reports or assessments. During this period the local education authority should not place the child in special education or unit, unless the parents consent.

The local education authority may hold meetings or case conferences to discuss any recommendations or issues. Parents should be informed of these, but do not necessarily have the right to attend.

Stage Five:

The assessment completed, the local education authority can: issue a statement, which will be issued in draft form to parents, and be accompanied by all the written evidence on which it is based. This should include the parents' evidence, including written notes by the local education authority officer of any oral input by the parents.

The local education authority will give the parents the name of a local education authority officer to go to for any further advice, not necessarily the same officer as before.

Parents have 15 days to comment, ask for meetings with people who have contributed to the statement, or visit any school named in the draft statement. Further meetings can be requested, each within 15 days of the last. This can be a protracted period, therefore, since there is no time limit in which the local education authority has to arrange the meeting. Local education authorities wishing to speed things may organise a big meeting involving all the professionals concerned. After the final meeting, parents have 15 days in which to comment

or

decide not to issue a statement: that is, decide the child has no special educational needs. This decision will be in writing, but may not give reasons. Parents have a right of appeal to the Secretary of

State, who can support the local education authority, or ask it to think again. He or she cannot agree with the parents.

Stage Six:

The final statement arrives. The local education authority will either confirm or amend the draft. If the parents agree with it, the local education authority will get on with implementing the provision set out in it. It is a statutory requirement that the provision listed in the statement is provided. It is therefore worth trying to get local education authorities to be precise about what they write.

'Speech therapy' can mean once in a school career.

'Small group' is open to interpretation.

If parents disagree with the statement, there is a procedure for appeal. This is heavily weighted in favour of the local education authority, so it is worth trying to negotiate agreement before that stage is reached. The first stage of appeal is to a local-education-authority-appointed committee. As if this were not biased enough, the local education authority does not have to abide by its decision anyway. The second stage of appeal is to the Secretary of State. The local education authority does have to abide by this decision, but there have been few parental success stories using the formal mechanism. More successful in achieving their goals have been those who simply refused point blank to use the school recommended, either at all, or unless certain conditions were met. The local education authority has the power to take the parents to court for refusing to send their children to school but it would be a brave local education authority that took the parents of a disabled child through the courts.

I am not advocating the latter course of action as the best. It is always preferable if a negotiated settlement can be reached at an earlier stage in the proceedings. Social workers help best who know the child, know the options, and know the law, and have skills in assertiveness and advocacy.

There are organisations to help. The most useful, all sadly in London, are the Children's Legal Centre, the Advisory Centre on Education and the Centre for Studies on Integration in Education, all of which are listed at the end of the book.

Stage Seven:

Statements are reviewed every twelve months, and a formal reassessment is done between the ages of twelve and a half years and fourteen and a half years. This triggers the proceedings for the social services to get formally involved under the Disabled Persons Act 1986. In the past, this was often the first contact families had with social services: The Children Act should rectify that over time.

FOSTER CARERS

Foster carers have rights, too, under The Education Act. The 1944 Education Act (Section 114) defined a parent as including a 'guardian and every person who has the actual custody of the child or young person'. In other words, the term parent covers not only the person having legal rights over the child, but the person having day-to-day care. Foster carers, therefore, have the right to be included in the decision making about the education of their foster child. They can request assessments, and contribute to them, they can be included in the statementing process, and have a right to see not only the statement but also all the written evidence on which it is based.

The Education Reform Act 1988

The Education Reform Act introduced the National Curriculum to schools, involving both a core and centrally determined common curriculum to schools, as well as a framework for testing pupils.

Disabled children were scarcely considered when the Bill was drafted, possibly because it was thought most such children would be in special schools and largely exempted. In practice, head teachers have to cope with a complex pattern of exemptions and modifications. Disability is a diverse phenomenon, and its accommodation in a set curriculum is bound to be fraught with dilemmas. Section 18 of the Act actually states that children statemented under the 1981 Act may be provided for in a way which

(a) excludes the application of provision of the National Curriculum, or

(b) does apply the National Curriculum but with such modifications as may be provided for in the statement.

Faced with the complexity of time-tabling, testing, maintaining staff morale, and interpreting regulations, head teachers may, perhaps, be forgiven for excluding children with disabilities because of the added inconvenience and extra effort their inclusion would require.

The National Curriculum is described in the introduction to the Act as one designed to promote 'spiritual, moral, cultural, mental and physical development of pupils at the school, and of society'. Precisely what is meant by 'and of society' is not clear, but it seems an ambitious goal. However, the philosophy is one of development of the whole child, and the inclusion of such facilities as speech and physiotherapy should not present any conceptual problems. This is not to deny the constant under-resourcing which plagues attempts to provide meaningful education for all children. Mainstream schools now have to demonstrate their effectiveness by maintaining high scores on national tests. This is likely to increase pressure not to include those disabled children who are likely to produce low scores, and bring the school's averages down. Such pupils are likely to be prejudged as 'failures' on the evidence of their disability, rather than their educational potential, which may be stifled before anyone has fairly explored it. This is not a good reason for shielding disabled children from the competition of mainstream schooling. Disabled children respond to competition in the same way as their able-bodied peers, as the successes of the group learning at Peto demonstrate. It is unfair competition which deprives children of any sense of achievement, which creates the tears and pain and causes children to stop trying, and parents, humiliated by their children's lack of success, to clamour for the shelter of a special school. Disabled children should be entitled to receive the same quality of education as other children, and the denial of access to the National Curriculum will ensure the continuation of an inferior offering. Special schools may shelter from the hurly-burly of mainstream schooling, but they teach social inferiority.

The Disabled Persons (Services, Consultation and Representation) Act 1986

The Education Act had provided a formal framework for identifying and assessing children in the education system with special needs. Although social services could be involved in the process of assessment, this only tended to happen when children were previously known to them and there were no formal arrangements for the sharing of responsibility with the education department. The intention of Sections 5 and 6 of the Disabled Persons Act 1986 was to bridge that gap and make the process of leaving school for the adult world a smoother process than had always been the case beforehand. Section 5, stripped to its bones, states that a local education authority must inform social services of the school leaving date of disabled children, and that social services must offer an assessment. Life is nothing if not complex however, and what should have been a simple process of continuation of concern for some of society's more vulnerable members has become in many cases a bureaucratic headache. In the first place, the groups covered by the Education Act and the 1986 Disabled Persons Act are different, meaning that not all children with special needs are disabled children covered by the 1986 Act.

The 1986 Disabled Persons Act defines a disabled person as

'A person to whom Section 29 of the National Assistance Act applies–i.e. people who are "blind, deaf or dumb, and other persons who are substantially and permanently handicapped by illness, injury or congenital deformity or who are suffering from a mental disorder within the meaning of the Mental Health Act"' (DHSS LAC 13/74).

A mental disorder is defined by Section 1 of the Mental Health Act 1983 as 'mental illness or incomplete development of mind, psychopathic disorder and any other disorder or disability of mind'.

The 1981 Act refers to children with special educational needs which result from either

'significantly greater difficulty in learning than the
    majority of children of their age'   or
'a disability which prevent them from making use of educational facilities of a kind generally provided'.

Clearly, this is a wider definition than that of disabled, under the 1986 Disabled Persons Act or the 1989 Children Act, both of which use the 1948 National Assistance Act definition. The decision about which children with special educational needs are included by the 1986 Act rests with the social services department. A department concerned to conserve resources, including that of its staff time, will seek to keep the definition tight. Any young person or family, or their professional advisers, who believe that a young person is missing out on resources by not being included, and therefore not being assessed, should challenge the social services decision, and ask for an assessment, either under Section 5 or, if the boat appears to have been missed, under Section 4 of the Act (see later).

Secondly, local education authorities are finding it administratively very difficult if not impossible to comply with the precise demands of the Act. This lays down that the local education authority informs social services eight months prior to the presumed leaving date of the child and (Section 6) keep the leaving date under review. The administrative systems of education departments are not geared up either to such predictions or to monitoring the changing intentions of their pupils. Often, no better than eligible leaving dates are available, i.e. sixteenth birthdays. Not everyone, of course, leaves school at the earliest possible opportunity and such dates are therefore not a sound basis for planning leavers assessments.

It has proved swifter and more accurate for social services departments to obtain the information from schools directly or from families concerned.

Thirdly, the 1986 Act gives no guide to what is meant by assessment, producing widely differing responses. Some social services departments have taken the view that, as disability is the prime issue, an occupational therapist's assessment is both appropriate and sufficient. Others have continued the Education Act pattern of a multi-disciplinary style assessment, with contributions from a number of professionals. The danger of too many such contributions is that some professionals will produce stilted assessments reminiscent of the worst kind of school report. Even in 1990, one medical officer of health produced a whole batch of assessments for a class of children all of which read—

'. . . . .is a pleasant child, who has had severe learning difficulties all of his life, and requires a special education'.

Such worthless contributions are not borne entirely of lack of concern or expertise, but of cynicism about a grinding bureaucracy, and a belief that nothing will be changed by the report, whatever is written.

If they are to do the child a service, social workers charged with dealing with assessments require an attitude which combines some healthy realism with a will to engineer change. This will be the more likely if the social worker concerned is not weighed down with too many routine, meaningless assessments of children for which social services will have no resources available, or who will make their way in the world without the need for social services resources. This is an issue for management. It is important that social workers in short supply are left free to concentrate on those children where intervention will most help and the interpretation of the definition of disabled is clearly the tool for restricting involvement to those families who will benefit from social work resources.

SECTION 4 of the 1986 Disabled Persons Act can also be relevant to children, although it is in many ways superseded by the Children Act. It clarifies that the local authority has a duty to assess the needs of any disabled person ordinarily resident in their area if the person requests it. The specific duty is to decide whether any of the provisions under the 1970 Chronically Sick and Disabled Persons Act apply. Section 2 of this Act provided a 'shopping list' or menu of services which could be provided by the local authority. They are detailed below. However, the Children Act allows for a wider package of services and social workers should not feel constrained by the 1970 Act menu.

SECTION 8 of the 1986 Disabled Persons Act places a duty on local authorities to take account of the ability of carers. There is a growing awareness of the problems faced by child carers, which should trigger local authorities to provide extra services.

SECTION 9 of the Act, as with the Children Act and the National Health Service and Community Care Act places a duty on local authorities to provide information about its services.

How this is achieved and how people are specifically targeted are dealt with in the next chapter on services.

Chronically Sick and Disabled Persons Act 1970

This has long been the foundation for local authority services for disabled people. Underfunding and 'lack of teeth' have both discredited the Act, and were reasons for the introduction of the Disabled Persons (Services, Consultation and Representation) Bill.

If the local authority is satisfied that a need exists, it can provide, under the Act—

a) practical assistance at home

b) assistance in obtaining a radio, or TV, library or other similar recreational facilities

c) lectures, games, outings or other recreational facilities outside the home, or assistance in taking advantage of educational facilities

d) assistance in travelling

e) adaptations to the home for safety, comfort or convenience

f) holidays

g) meals

h) telephones, or equipment to make use of them.

This chapter has dealt with the main pieces of legislation relating specifically to disabled children. It has demonstrated it is not a simple arena, and as such favours those who are energetic, articulate and assertive, or who have advocates with such qualities. There are clear roles for rights workers in such a field, whether these are from local authorities, with obvious risks of clashes of interests, voluntary organisations or independent advocacy schemes.

It is important, however, in addressing the specialist law relating to disability, that disabled children are also included within all the other child care law that exists, and which I am not, for reasons both of space and duplication, going to repeat here. Decisions concerning disabled children should be based firstly on their needs as children: for stability, security, protection. Any decision-making that places the needs of the disability first is denying a very basic human right. Since 1991, this has also been a legal right.

6. SERVICES

THE EXTENT OF DISABILITY

Articles on the state of any service traditionally begin with an overview of the demographic situation and it would undoubtedly reassure many readers if I could offer the same. The problem is that the number of disabled children is not known with any accuracy, partly because of a lack of comprehensive registers and partly because of a lack of agreement about what constitutes a disability. In other words, much depends on the interpretation of the definition, as well as which definition is used. Most definitions of disability are open to interpretation, particularly where children or old people are concerned.

The World Health Organisation, for example, defines disability as:

any restriction or lack (resulting from an impairment) of ability to perform an activity in the manner or within the range considered normal for a human being.

Whereas it may be normal for a 40-year-old to run up a flight of stairs without panting, would it be so for an 80-year-old? More pertinent, given the subject of this book, is to ask whether the 80-year-old is disabled by age, or by the step builder?

The OPCS surveys of disability in Britain in 1989, using the above WHO definition, estimated that in 1985 a total of 286,000 5-15-year-olds were disabled, 56,000 of them severely (OPCS 1989). A year later the DES estimated some 135,380 pupils were subjects of statements of special educational need. (House of Commons Select Committee 1987.)

Not all disabled children, in other words, have special educational needs. Neither, given the experience of social work departments assessing school-leavers, are all statemented children disabled.

My own conception of this confusion is a picture of two overlapping circles, one representing disabled children, according to social services, the other children in need of special education.

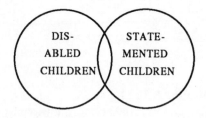

To add to this confusion, the health services in any area are likely to be dealing with yet another group. Such definitions, and consequent attempts to categorise groups of people, feed the requirements of bureaucracy, and are of little obvious value to individuals with specific needs. Labelling, moreover, is stigmatic. Having extra help with reading is one thing. Being labelled as in need of special education is quite another. Future planning, usually given as the reason to maintain registers, would be more accurately based on measurements of unmet demand for services than it is on subjective interpretations of disability and the crude numbers on registers.

Although the current picture is chaotic, some general trends can still be identified: marginalisation, difficulty of access, lack of co-ordination, and low opinions of social work.

Marginalisation

Disabled children are marginalised from the principal function of welfare organisation. The health service marginalises disabled children because it cannot cure them. The education service marginalises them because it is geared to putting as many children as possible through its examination sausage machine. The focus of child protection services is able-bodied children. The social services elderly and physically handicapped sections focus on adults. There is even a common belief that disabled children are more properly the responsibility of health and education services until they are grown up. Disabled children are thus categorised as sick, educationally special, or handicapped. Parents find themselves deskilled by a plethora of experts, all of whom do their bit and pass the case on for the next part of the child's problem to be dealt with.

Few services can produce any long term plans for disabled children. Local authorities, in particular, can move exceedingly slowly because of the demands of the committee cycles. It is important to remember, however, that it is local authorities, not social services departments, who are charged with implementing the Children Act. While this opens the way for imaginative use of resources, it remains to be seen how long it takes for imagination to translate itself into action.

Difficult Access

One of the most striking things found, after setting up a new multi-disciplinary team to assess the resource needs of school-leavers, was that the overwhelming majority had had no previous contact with social services departments (Sefton Social Services, 1990). Some, of course, did not want it, either then or previously, but most questioned the rationale of a service that was offering itself years too late.

Parents were surveyed by the Sefton Social Services team after the first year of offering assessments to school-leavers. They were asked what they thought about our initial approach, and how it might have been better. While one or two suggested displaying material in public places, such as post offices, could be helpful, the majority view was that people needed to be sure the information was directed at THEM. If it did not actually land on their door-mat with their name on it, they were unlikely to identify with it or respond. This message seems to justify the passing on of information about individuals from one organisation to another, such as health to social services, in order that direct approaches can be made to offer help and explain possibilities. There is a need to be more sensitive to what parents actually want.

There is a vicious circle here. Social work is usually a *re*active, not a *pro*active activity. Parents repeatedly state a preference for professionally initiated visiting, so that they are not obliged to think of a particular problem, or have a crisis, to legitimate asking. (Glendinning, 1983.) Such a scenario conveniently lets social work off the hook. Furthermore, should a parent ask for something that is not provided, and is therefore told the resource is unavailable, they are unlikely to call again. Worse, they may be made to feel that even the act of asking was wrong. Receptionists can be as scathing as professional staff. Authorities can then claim there is no demand yet it is only by generating demand that there can ever be any increase in services.

Cumbersome as they are, the assessments under the 1986 Disabled Persons Act can at least provide a means of generating demand. So far, unlike the statementing under the 1981 Education Act, there does not seem to be undue organisational pressure on staff to only produce assessments in terms of available resources.

Bearing in mind the conditioning most disabled youngsters receive to be grateful and not make a fuss, social workers may find themselves in the business of opening minds to possibilities and encouraging the raising of expectations. Even if they cannot always be met, raised expectations are the engines of progress.

It is not always necessary to encourage individuals to raise their horizons. Some already know what they need and what they want. There may be a problem in their communicating it. Social services departments, despite being in the communication business, are often more skilled at rationing. At a very basic level, reception in social work offices leaves a great deal to be desired. Consumers are treated as potential threats, having limited comfort or seating. So long as social work continues to stigmatise its consumers as second class citizens, people will hesitate to approach them for advice or help. The assumption of many reception staff that clients are scroungers to be deterred rather than encouraged results in only the very desperate ever crossing the threshold. Talking to people through grilles or holes in glass does not inspire confidence. The culture of the organisation which the receptionists transmit is an issue for management. An alternative route for parents of younger children is through groups at resource centres or child development centres. The rationing procedure is not nearly so stringent as at an area office, but requires an acceptance that their child has a disability, or special needs. Resource centres are a great deal more welcoming than most area offices, and any parental cliques that develop do at least pass with the years.

Lack of Co-ordination

In a report on social work with disabled children, Glendinning described the unco-ordinated nature of services. (Glendinning, 1986.) A family might be visited and advised by a profusion of different professionals from different agencies, with different criteria for service, different application methods, different concepts and terms, and different ways to appeal. Professionals who were flexible and expected to use their discretion did not help, since there were no rules to go on. Parents felt undermined by having to ask for discretionary services and risk being turned down.

The situation has not changed. No single agency takes responsibility, but many are involved: medical staff; health visitors; psychologists; speech therapists; nurseries; occupational therapists; voluntary organisations; Family Fund staff; DSS; careers officers; DROs; DAS staff; Rehabilitation officers, keyworkers.

Therefore disabled children rarely receive a service through mainstream area offices. There is a range of other options: some areas being better served than others. Some children with learning disabilities will be included in the remit of community mental handicap teams, which have a largely adult clientele, and a medical focus. Many parents are rightly wary of identifying their young children as mentally handicapped. Some areas will have child development centres, usually either based in hospitals or jointly funded by the health service. These typically cater for under fives, and are staffed on a multi-disciplinary basis. The usual model is a medical one. Glendinning reports that social work intervention, since the child is unable to be cured, 'may be little more than an amelioration of the practical and emotional stresses of this long term dependency'. (Glendinning,1986 p.17). Funding constraints cause difficulties here as in other areas of welfare, leading to limited opening hours, poor facilities and a reliance on donations for much equipment. Nevertheless, reports from parents are usually favourable, if not at the time, certainly with hindsight from the comparative wilderness of the poorer services to come.

The Children Act encourages the development of resources for under fives. Section 18 imposes a duty on all local authorities to provide such day care for children in need who are aged five and under, and such care and supervised activity out of school and during school holidays for children in need who are over five. It spoils things a little by adding 'as appropriate' to its mandate. Social work support is available in hospital departments. While there are undoubtedly experts in such departments, for many families the centralisation of children's hospital services means it is a case of too little at too great a distance. Long term support from locally based community services is often lacking, as hospital-based workers complain there is nowhere to refer on to. As with community workers, priority is given to child protection. It is possible that with independent management of hospitals some local authorities will choose to reduce or pull out altogether from social work provision.

Views About Social Workers

Caroline Glendinning reported that one parent felt the social worker was only interested in whether or not her child was alive or not: a feature perhaps of the 'Watch Your Back' mentality which has grown up in some beleaguered departments. (Glendinning, 1983.) More widespread complaints concerned lack of information, the inability to do anything practical, the onus on parents to make contact, high staff turnover, generic rather than specialist staff. Parents recognised the pressure social workers were under, and many seemed to have internalised their low priority status to the extent that they failed to question this. Social workers are clearly quite good at letting people know how busy they are. CCETSW also found that social workers with disabled people frequently lacked the knowledge and skills to do the job. (CCETSW, 1974.) The lessons for social work, and social work management, from these service users are fairly straightforward. People need to be given more time: using an appointment system can aid time management and reduce wasted visiting time. Routine visiting, even at lengthy intervals, is a user preference. It relieves them of having to have a reason for a visit, coping without support or inventing a crisis. Social workers need to be well informed, and to share the information. Finally, it is unhelpful to keep telling people how busy you are.

Social Workers and Power

The Children Act places a duty on local authorities to provide services to minimise the effects of disability. This should not be seen simply in terms of aids in the home. It means providing the means of independent mobility and effective communication. It also means aiding children to value themselves, to have ambitions, to manage discrimination, and, as they get older, to advocate on their own behalf. This approach requires social workers firstly to advocate on their behalf, and the skills required in such an activity are discussed later. More basic, however, is an outlook that regards the social work task as negotiating the best deal with and for the child, without rendering either the child or the parents dependent. This entails a willingness to share both skills and information, as well as taking on individuals and organisations, where appropriate, on the child's behalf. This is empowerment.

Empowerment has become a fashionable concept, and there are certainly some who would argue that giving power is patronising in its own way. Social workers are powerful people, and in many cases the best service they can offer to disabled children and their parents is to share some of that power.

The influence of the medical mystique, maintained on the dubious assumption that information about their own or their child's condition is bad for people, is obvious. This is not to suggest that information is forced on people, but the right to know as much as the worker should be acknowledged. Less commonly recognised are the powerful skills that social workers have. Some basic advice on how to deal with other organisations or departments is a valuable resource, reusable by the person concerned. Passing on such tricks-of-the-trade to users, and so moving away from a client-professional into a sharing relationship is unlikely to appeal to professionals who need the status gap, or who need to be needed, but it is an essential step in recognising users as fellow citizens. The best discovery from such an approach will be that the process is a two-way one.

Effective and efficient social workers are those with the knowledge and skills to make things happen. The next stage is for them to pass on their trade secrets.

Dealing with Poverty

Poverty is a depressing problem with which to deal. Budget planning is something of a nonsense where the real problem is usually a shortage of funds, but attention to welfare rights can improve a family's finances. Local authorities have the power to provide loans, but these can in themselves prove a burden since they have to be paid back. A local authority should, however, be a better bet than a loan shark. Loans are subject to means testing, but people on income support will be eligible. There are a range of benefits and concessions available where a child in the family is disabled. Indeed many poor families rely heavily for day-to-day funds on benefits designed to alleviate care or mobility needs of disabled children. For severely disabled children under sixteen, the Family Fund can provide assistance in the form of grants for various pieces of equipment, such as washing machines, or holidays. Contrary to popular opinion, this is not a charity, although it is administered by the Rowntree Trust, and parents of severely disabled children should be encouraged to apply for help as of right. There are, of course, a range of charities who can offer help in the form of cash or in kind. Many of the better services for disabled children are provided by charities, whatever one may think of their sometimes degrading fund-raising methods. People give their money voluntarily to charity to benefit disabled children, and it is a matter of parental choice whether or not to seek aid from such sources. Social workers who oppose charity on principle, and deny 'their clients' the knowledge of their existence, are being equally patronising, in denying the disabled person the right to choose.

Helping People Deal with the Education Department

Let us take the scenario of a family with a child about to start the process of having an assessment made by the education department. The parents want their child in a particular school with additional resources to those provided as standard. Inevitably, meetings with the education department are in the offing, plus much paperwork. The social worker can share her knowledge of the procedures. She can give the family a copy of the ACE handbook, if they want it, or a more simplified guide. (ACE 1983.) She can prepare the family for a potentially long period of negotiation.

It is useful with some parents to offer very basic advice, even if it is sometimes hard to follow. Confrontation, particularly as a first move, rarely has the desired outcome, since both sides quickly become entrenched. Advise politeness, but firmness. Suggest that insulting or shouting at the education officer will not help. Neither will banging on the table or slamming the door. As with most advice, this is easier to offer than to take. I remain humbled by the memory of coaching one very volatile parent in the need not to lose her temper in a meeting, and then losing my own. She was rightly very puzzled when we left, and her 'I thought you said we weren't to shout!', still haunts me. On a practical note, the family should be advised to open and keep their own file on their child. This could even be provided by the social services department. Copies of all correspondence can then be stored. Carbon paper may be a little messy, but it is not expensive. All letters to the local education authority should be dated, to ease follow up either by letter or telephone call. Saying 'I wrote to you on 4th August' is always preferable to 'I wrote a while ago'. It conveys the additional message that you are keeping a record. In a meeting a file is a useful prop, for the same reason, even if it is not opened. It gives a clear non-verbal message that the family are organised and mean business. Any telephone messages should also be logged on the file, with the date, the name of the caller, if possible, and roughly what was said. If the caller refuses a name—unusual for education departments, although the DSS still retain the practice—this should be noted too. These can be referred to later.

Meetings with the local education authority can be formidable, and parents and young people can be helped to survive and get what they want by some advice, or even a practice run, beforehand. This is not to suggest social workers opt out of the meeting, but their role should become more supportive and less representative. In the end, many young people can become their own advocates.

The local education officers have a lot more experience of meetings than many service users, and are on their own territory.

Some skilled and confident parents may overcome these obstacles but the power balance is usually with the authority. Parents should be advised to take along their file, plus a list of points, sorted out beforehand, of what they want to cover. They should ask the meeting to pause while they make any notes they require, so that it goes at their pace, not the speed of the local education authority. If necessary, they should request an adjournment while they consult: parent with parent, or with the social worker, or with the young person. They should be prepared to be patient, and to sit through the distractions of dirty tricks which are sometimes used. Some are plain inefficiency. Others seem more deliberate attempts to be off-putting. Delayed starts are commonplace. Talking about matters which are irrelevant is another, as is the practice of talking at length about the problems of the school, or the local education authority or the council in general.

Such deviations should be recognised for what they are, and pointed out to the local education officers. . .'that's all very interesting, but I'm here to discuss what you are doing for my child'. Patience is bound to be required and it is as well to prepare people. Meetings can be short if everyone agrees, but are inevitably longer if there are differences. The bum-in-the chair technique has much to commend it. If possible, simply do not move until you have achieved something. Sit with your back to the door, so the others cannot easily escape, and go easy on the tea and coffee.

This means knowing what you want in the first place. Too many people are disappointed by the outcome of meetings because they have not clearly thought out their own agenda beforehand. It is important that all the people representing the child are agreed on their objectives. Nothing destroys a family's case faster than mother and father disagreeing in front of the education officers. Wants should be realistic, but there is nothing wrong with having a preference, as well as a fall back position: what you will settle for. This is a basic negotiating skill.

At the outset of a meeting both sides should state their positions, and establish exactly what is being discussed. It does not help if the family and the local education authority are working to different agendas. Local education authorities should not be allowed to get away with establishing the family's position without setting out their own. It is also important to find out who is at the meeting, not just by name, but their positions. If no one is taking notes, write them yourself.

Recording anything important that is said is a good idea. Even being seen to take notes will dissuade the local education authority from inventing their own minutes later. Most social workers will have experienced reading minutes of meetings which bear scant resemblance to the actual event. Yet it is the minutes which become the reality at a later date. Get the parents to check the notes back with the officers to ensure that they agree on their accuracy. Try to get someone's signature. If not, a social worker or other representative or friend who is present will act as a witness. Advise any lone parents against attending unaccompanied. Any friend will do. There is no need to speak: only to stay awake and look intelligent.

Listening to Children

Social workers have a role in representing the interests of children. Sadly, this is not always the same as that of the parents, and there may be an argument for two workers where conflict is serious. However, a more usual failing is not taking full account of a child's view. It is much easier for able-bodied social workers to relate to able-bodied parents than it is for either of them to understand the point of view of a disabled child. Disabled adults may fare better, but there remains a temptation to assume the grown-ups know best.

This is not to suggest that the responsibilities for decisions should be placed on shoulders too young either to want them or to cope with them. It is to suggest a conscious effort to communicate with young children, and to involve them more and more fully as they grow older.

Social workers also have a role in encouraging a belief in children of their own self worth. A career in disability can be a process of learning to be second class. A child is not born with an inferiority complex nor with a disabled identity but both of these are easily cultivated in a society which does not readily tolerate differences. Listening to children is a seriously underdeveloped skill and becomes more so when the children are disabled. We often do not really know what they think, because we do not ask them and expect their parents to represent them instead.

Respite Care

One area where the tensions are evident, and children's views do not always seem to come first, is that of respite care. Respite means having a break from caring and is modelled on adults caring for other adults who become disabled or chronically sick. The term 'respite' implies relief from a burden, and awareness of this has led some organisations to use 'natural break' or 'short-stay' to emphasise normality. Respite usually occurs in residential units or hospitals, on an erratic or planned basis. More rarely, assistance for carers is provided in the home, although this is still more likely to be through an agency such as Crossroads than through the local authority. Where caring for disabled children is concerned the pattern is usually for the child to be taken from the home to give the parents a break. At worse, this is hospital: no place to be if you are not ill. The alternatives are in a residential home or with a foster family as part of a scheme variously called Family Link or Shared Care. Parents in most areas ask for help in their own home in vain. Only the rich can afford a nanny.

A scheme of planned respite has proved a very attractive social worker's option. Great efforts are made to arrange and book the residential home or substitute family, introduce the child, and prepare the family. Having gone through this painstaking process, social workers may well be surprised to discover that the child does not actually go at the appointed time. The social worker gets irritated, the family get distressed. They have been made to feel the answer is there, and they are wrong not to take it. Yet, it is not usual for young children to spend nights away from home, except with close relatives. Parents' ambivalence at such a 'solution' to their difficulties is scarcely surprising. It also, of course, questions both their skill and their responsibility, as parents. Even when respite does occur, there is evidence that many children do not like being sent away. They wet the bed, they report nightmares, or cry for their mother. All of these phenomena are what might be expected from any young child who is homesick, and yet an increased effort is made for children seen as being a burden at home to get over their homesickness, for their parents' sake.

In her study of respite schemes in Lothian, Stalker reports that of the thirty children studied, eleven experienced marked homesickness, which in some cases was persistent and severe. (Stalker, 1987.) Such behaviour as refusal to return to carers, crying and screaming, wanting to go to bed to avoid leaving home, refusal to eat during visits, temper tantrums, inability to sleep, making himself sick, constant whingeing and a refusal to engage with mother are all instances from the study.

Social workers pay a great deal of attention to preparing parents for 'letting go', and remain surprised that some parents are just as stressed by the respite experience as by caring at home. By the time the child is prepared, the anxiety worked through, and the time 'made up' by the guilty parent when the child returns, there is hardly anything left. Robinson notes that many parents and siblings of users of respite schemes miss them. (Robinson, 1986.) Of course they do. Robinson also reports difficulties for children in adapting to respite. Despite regular and frequent visits to carer's family homes some children never stayed overnight. Most of the parents in the study thought their children enjoyed their stays with foster families, although nearly half reported their children were upset. 29% said their children were homesick while away and a further 9% did not know. 73% experienced anxiety or guilt while their child was away.

Looking instead at the children's reactions, Robinson reports disturbed behaviour similar to that reported by Stalker: withdrawal, hiding luggage, tears, kicking and screaming. (Robinson, 1987.)

These findings reflect those of Oswin in children using residential short term facilities. (Oswin 1984.) It is important to recognise that children with learning disabilities experience the same feelings of distress as any other child when separated from their parents, and, while we move heaven and earth to keep non-disabled children with their families where possible, the very opposite rule seems to apply where the child has a disability. Despite all this evidence, there has been a persistent belief that respite is a 'good thing', and that all that is necessary is to find ways of reducing the stress and overcoming parental and children's reluctance. Generally speaking the focus of respite is to meet the needs of carers and it is less often a valued experience for the disabled person, be she adult or child.

It is true that many parents manage only because of the relief of respite, and that many carers also get a great deal from it. It is therefore a valuable resource, but only if the child feels the same way about it. If not, and bearing in mind the high percentage of parents feeling anxious and guilty about it, it seems high time some other means of helping parents to care were worked out. Why, then, do we persist in pushing respite care for young children as a resource for parents raising a disabled child, rather than offering it merely as one option? Stalker notes that a number of parents applied to join the Lothian Share Care Scheme because they had been persuaded by professionals. (Stalker, 1987.) The truth is probably that it is often the only 'solution' in the bag, which reflects the backward state of services for disabled children.

None of this is to suggest that respite does not work for some, and is not an important service. It does, however, highlight the danger of having only one resource and assuming that, with a little persuasion, it will suit everyone. In considering respite, especially for young children, professionals should ask themselves the following questions.

Is removing the child the first choice of the parent, or all I can think of? Would the parent consider removal, if there was an alternative?

Would I be considering the same solution if the child were able-bodied and the mother reporting stress?

Is the child trying to communicate something by her behaviour, and should I not be responding?

If the answers to these questions suggest a different kind of resource to that on the local authority's shelves it is the social worker's job to try and create something new or to negotiate a package with a voluntary organisation to provide it. A common request received when working with parents of severely disabled young children is for sitters, who will come to their home for a day, or a few hours, while they go out. These are not home helps so much as carers at home. In some cases, it is possible to engage local baby sitting circles, once the problem of lack of reciprocity is dealt with. This often means reassuring people who are frightened of 'handicap' although cash helps too. In less straightforward circumstances, local volunteer bureaux can be tapped, and expenses provided by charitable sources. What is really required, though, is some effective lobbying of local councillors to provide moneys for paying people to care. This would be a reasonable extension of current foster care services in the children's section of a local authority, although the term 'fostering' probably is unhelpful in this context and would involve the same standard checks. Currently, respite services are as likely to be provided under an adult-based service, or as part of the Community Mental Handicap Initiatives with the health service. These arrangements serve to segregate disabled children from other children.

Institutional Disablism and Ways of Tackling It

In Chapter 3 on Screening, I did not give much consideration to social services departments. They have, of course, behaved no differently than the rest of society. Those services which exist for disabled children have often been provided separately from those for other children, in hospital departments (reinforcing the sick role) or through voluntary organisations (reinforcing a reliance on charity). Worse, they are provided as the poorest relation of the Cinderella services for disabled adults, usually further split between those who have a physical or sensory disability and those with a learning disability. The Children Act makes it quite clear that services for all children in need should be integrated. This is an issue for managers in social services departments to rectify, but for others to demand.

For the rest, an alternative to the current situation whereby society stigmatises and devalues disabled people will not emerge overnight. It might seem impossible for social workers to have any effect on society's organisation and structures. Nevertheless, the magnitude of the task has not prevented organisation and action in other fields. The barrier is perhaps less a feeling of helplessness than a failure to recognise that the oppression of disabled people, called apartheid by some, is an issue as vital as tackling racism and sexism. As a profession social work has a vital role at the frontiers of thinking. The task is to find ways of redrawing the boundary lines, so that the label of 'disabled' does not create an automatic, and compulsory, difference in service provision and to think in terms of the potential, rather than the problems, of disabled children.

The Social Services Inspectorate suggested that disabled people require more adult-to-adult related services. (DHSS 1988.) Services which treat adults as children reflect both the medical model, which treats ALL sick people as if they are four-year-olds, and the reluctance to accept disabled people as full citizens, or disabled children as citizens of the future.

Professionals who accord users dignity and respect their opinions are more likely to be staff who have respect and dignity themselves. It is harder for people who are themselves at the bottom of the pecking order, low paid, undervalued and downtrodden, with little discretion, to accord others any respect. If people are expected to work in crummy, dirty offices, and to interview people in uncarpeted, dark little rooms or corridors both worker and user are degraded, and feel unimportant. This can lead to individuals exercising what little control they have to the fullest possible extent, however petty and irritating it might be. On the other hand, if disabled users can discuss their needs with people who have the authority to meet them, this is of direct benefit to the users.

A political dimension is added by the disability movement which is challenging perceptions through various organisations run by disabled people. Many professionals working within the disability field welcome the existence of such organisations, particularly if they are prepared to take on councils or voluntary bodies, as they generate energy and pressure for improvements. Nothing is more depressing for a worker seeking to improve services and develop opportunities than to be operating in an area where there are no organisations of disabled people, or where the only ones consist of a band of grateful disabled people who expect nothing more than a turkey dinner at Christmas and bingo the rest of the year. Many disabled people are too ready to allow able-bodied people to run their organisations and represent them to the powers that be. The low expectations of many young people growing up with disabilities is depressing, even if it is understandable. A user group at a local day centre, encouraged to make plans and proposals for the use of the centre by a new manager, took a year to suggest tentatively that the colour of the bus was wrong. This reflects a lifetime of conditioning into submission. Disabled children need to be able from the earliest possible age to express their opinions, unless the pattern is to repeat itself in the next generation.

There are a number of aims that can be worked on. All except the very youngest children could be involved in any case conferences or reviews held about them. Older children can be helped to chair their own conferences. Children in long-term care in children's homes could be involved in staff selection. This is not the same as transferring the responsibility, but involves children more closely in choice about who looks after them.

Involving users in planning day services or youth training schemes carries the danger that the users are not as progressive as the management hope. A new manager at an adult training centre for young people with learning disabilities run on traditional lines, introduced a whole package of educational programmes and tried to end the contract packing jobs she considered exploitative and degrading. The loud radio was turned off to allow people to talk to each other. The users did not argue and all seemed to be going smoothly until she set up a users committee who eventually expressed a wish to go back to packing soap, as many of them liked doing it and did not want to broaden their minds. She found this impossible to accept and resisted for a long time on the grounds that the youngsters were conditioned into accepting routine and boring tasks, and would soon see she was right. Asking what people want is pointless unless you are prepared to accept the answers.

Disabled people are increasingly used as trainers, and should be paid properly to do it, as well as receiving instruction in teaching methods and educational tricks of the trade, if only to avoid boring the audience. Disabled people who can only describe their own disability do not take the issue very far. Disabled people should also be employed as access officers and advisers to the planning department, if only on a sessional basis to incorporate advice from a range of disability groups. It is too easy to assume that disabled people will both train and advise on disability matters out of the goodness of their hearts. Being treated as an equal means being paid the going rate. All these aims involve the relinquishing of power by professional workers. This is not simply an act of will. There is a need to recognise that social problems, including those where disability is a factor, are not individual pathologies, but a part of the power structures of society. Assessment is all too often an assessment of the individual (popularly dubbed an MOT) and intervention programmes or action plans are all too often similarly limited in scope. The popularity of 'individual programme planning' reflects this focus on individual need, as opposed to the rights or entitlements denied to whole sections of society.

The recognition that 'community care' is based on the maintenance of women as carers either as family members or as low-paid staff is important. Care is regarded as the 'natural' function of women, unless there is a war or a temporary shortage in the labour market, when crèches suddenly spring up like mushrooms on a damp morning. Home helps, home carers, wardens, day care assistants etc. are part of the exploitative pattern of low pay with no career structure. Both family carers and paid carers are usually under stress and overworked, yet Glenys Jones reports they are more likely to be in conflict than supporting each other. (Jones, 1989.) This is a management issue. Low-aid workers in stressful jobs require considerably more support than is currently the case. Workload management and stress management should not just be for higher paid professionals. Home helps and wardens can be working in very isolated situations yet encounter just as much human pain as social workers with a supervision structure and the support of a team of colleagues. Most home help organisers would envy the supervisory ratios common to social work. Family carers too require more support. The rights of disabled children have to be reconciled with the rights of women carers. If women who care feel ground down and exhausted by the task, this is passed on to the children - as resentment, irritation, guilt, or even as physical abuse and neglect. Carers up to their arm-pits in dirty nappies are unlikely to be receptive to ideas about child development.

Unless such basic issues are addressed, community care will represent no advance for disabled people, but more of the same poor quality service. The rights of women carers are not incompatible with the rights of children, and the rights of disabled children should become part of the agenda of the women's movement. Social workers have not been encouraged to be political. The Barclay Report on social work actually recommended that social workers 'have to accept the decisions the authority takes or, if they see an unsupportable conflict between their clients' interests and the authority's policy, move to other jobs'. (Barclay Report 1982.) It did not explain where this left the client. A disabled person employed by a local authority would face the same pressure to take the corporate view and not make demands on behalf of users that contradicted council policy.

There are two routes around this dilemma, neither of which can an individual effectively travel alone. One is a strengthening of professional organisations, such as The British Association of Social Workers (BASW) or trade unions to empower and protect professional workers threatened by their own employers. This requires these organisations to set their own agendas for improving services for disabled children. A second is the active involvement of organisations of disabled people, not simply as vociferous critics but as organisations with the power and authority to effect changes. As far as children are concerned, many adult disability organisations have yet to find a way to properly represent them. Both of these routes have yet to be fully explored.

ISSUES FOR SOCIAL WORK MANAGEMENT

There is little point identifying the social work tasks in relation to disabled children unless there is also recognition in management of the support and training that are required.

Throughout the course of this book I have picked out various strands to the social work task. I have described it in terms of sharing skills and information, empowerment, involving users, and acting as an advocate. I have mentioned that there is a political dimension when professional considerations and users' interests do not coincide with bureaucratic demands or traditional resources. I have further emphasised that social work with families with a disabled or sick child is emotionally draining and time consuming, particularly if the child dies.

I have highlighted parents' comments about social workers being of no practical help, changing too often, and not taking the initiative. Recognition that working with disabled children is skilful, time consuming and stressful has obvious implications for management, from selection of staff to their support and training. Specialist staff require controlled caseloads, access to information technology and technicians, and attractive packages to encourage people to stay around a little longer.

Issues for First Line Management

At first line management level there is a need to validate the emotional reactions of workers, while at the same time ensuring these are kept within some sort of proportion. Empathy is one thing: hi-jacking the experience of the disabled child or parent quite another. Social workers with disabilities themselves may need particular support, to ensure their own feelings about their situation and childhood do not become confused with, or imposed upon, those of the service user. While their common experience of oppression is valid, and the route to understanding clearer, it is essential to avoid making assumptions that the commonality of a disability results in the same needs. A disabled social worker can be as guilty of stereotyping as the next person.

Whether they welcome the prospect or not, a disabled worker provides a role model for young disabled people, and this can be a mixed blessing. The young person cannot so readily insist on their own incapabilities, or fall back on their disability, when faced with a disabled social worker. The role they have learned, as a child, of a disabled person as the object of sympathy and the disability as the problem, is challenged by the disabled person holding down a professional job. A disabled worker, say, driving a car, is much more likely to be able to raise the sights of school-leavers into asking more of and for themselves. Not everyone, however, wants to rise to the challenge, resulting in requests for another social worker. This sometimes comes from parents, but occasionally from youngsters themselves who have internalised a belief that disabled means second best. Disabled workers needs backing and support in that situation to clarify their reactions. In particular, there may be feelings from the worker of disloyalty and rejection, as expectations of other disabled people can run high. The worker, who will undoubtedly have struggled against the odds to be in the job, may feel the need to have all the answers, especially with a disabled service user. Understanding human behaviour is not easy and the disabled worker often requires more security in order to ask for guidance than a confident able-bodied person. Some understanding of why the service user has rejected the worker is necessary to help the worker deal with the frustration, and go back. Social services departments do not usually respond to requests for a change of worker, rightly or wrongly, and there is no justification for doing so on the grounds that the worker has a disability, any more than if the worker is a woman or is black, or is all three. It is important that the agency develops clear policies on handling disablist service users, whether they are themselves disabled or not.

It is also essential that social workers for disabled children are competent, whether they are disabled or otherwise, and there is no justification for employing someone with a disability who has no potential or any abilities in the social work field.

Workload management is also an issue for management, and is, of course, a balancing act. Recognition that the work can sometimes involve considerable emotional strain means that management legitimise, even encourage, release of stress. Some workers will have sufficient release mechanisms in their out-of-work life to need little attention to easing stress at work. In other cases, social work teams will deal with the matter internally both by skylarking and by providing shoulders to cry on. There will always be some staff, particularly those working in relative isolation, who have neither outlet, and who stoically store up stress until it becomes a major problem. Disabled workers can be especially vulnerable because of the additional pressures they put upon themselves to succeed, and not to make mistakes. These issues apply not simply to social work staff, or other professional workers, but also to the telephonists and reception staff, who bear much of the pain and anger of the parents and children. Workload management is a tool for keeping stress levels down by not overfacing workers. In some areas, the bombardment of referrals can be very high, and workers who are made to feel responsible for the long waiting lists are being unfairly treated. Waiting lists can often be managed more efficiently although it is usually a case of too few workers.

Priorities must be set, in this as any other field, but they should include respect for the worker. This means building in time for long term work, training, and recharging batteries, as well as responding to new enquirers. The last mentioned can be contacted by letter or telephone if the wait is likely to be prolonged, which maintains respect for enquirers without shielding them from the reality of shortages. It is better to respond by letter promising, and keeping, an appointment six weeks hence than it is to ignore the person altogether as so often happens. In times of serious staff shortage, where no response can be made at all, it is only courteous to tell the person why no one will be coming.

A two stream system of workload management whereby a certain amount of time is devoted to 'assessment' and a certain amount to long term work, ensures the worker does not get bogged down with assessment with no follow up nor respond to new referrals because of established caseloads. Long term work itself requires review, and should include a contract with the user to achieve agreed goals. This not only makes more sense than an open-ended contract, it is more honest than dropping people when other demands become too insistent. With children, the contract may well involve a regular visit initiated by the worker. This is often a parental preference, but it should not be adopted as a matter of routine with all families. All too often social work with disabled people has deteriorated into a pattern of visiting with no clear purpose and no plans for action. Some families have no idea what the worker is doing there One single parent reported that her local authority social worker called a great deal, and drank a lot of coffee. This caused a not insignificant dent in her budget, particularly as she herself drank only tea. It is up to managers to make sure social workers visit with a reason, and that the user shares it.

It saves time to visit by appointment. It may be hard to be precise, but giving people a morning, afternoon or evening is usually workable, especially since these definitions are elastic. The disadvantage for the user can be in terms of the need to tidy up, since the visit is not a surprise, and the necessity of cancelling when workers are sick. Not everyone is on the telephone, although the days when social work clients were, by definition, too poor to be on the telephone are long gone.

Issues for Senior Management

Clearly, if progress is to be made in any broad sense, there are moves that senior management should be taking, other than adopting a permissive attitude toward the kind of working described - sharing information and skills, working with consumers, supporting staff and managing workloads. Senior managers clearly have to take responsibility for quality assurance as well as ensuring that proper complaints procedures are in force for when things go wrong. This means looking not only at the procedures for dissatisfaction to be expressed directly, but for working with advocates. In the unimplemented sections 1 and 2 of the 1986 Disabled Persons Act, provision for representation for disabled consumers was made. The Section was never implemented, but such practice is widely viewed as progressive. It is not actually necessary to have an Act in order to involve users, take complaints seriously, and make use of representation or advocacy schemes. The Children Act requires the local authority to establish a procedure for representations, including complaints, about the discharge of its duties under Part III. This includes identification, assessment, promoting children's welfare, preventing suffering and neglect, providing day care and accommodation. The procedure should have some independent element. At the time of writing detailed procedures were still awaited but it can be assumed this opens the way for either professional representatives or advocacy schemes. Again, there is no need to wait for the law to institute good practice. This is not as simple as just setting up procedures. It is well known that consumers of social services rarely complain. Added to this awareness should be the particular lack of confidence, and possible difficulties in communication, experienced by many disabled children and young people. Any complaints procedure that does not address these issues is worth little.

Senior management need also to take some responsibility for ending the current second rate, segregated system by which disabled children get any service. Although it stigmatises disabled children by specifying a register, the Children Act also makes it clear that services should be integrated. This means making services part and parcel of services for children, not afterthoughts in an adult and physically handicapped, or health related, mental health, or hospital division. The strategic aims should be to end the piecemeal nature of the service, to fund it directly rather than rely on bits of other people's budgets, to raise the status of staff working with disabled children so that it becomes an attractive career option. Rather than adapting adult services to take account of children, services should be planned by putting children first from the outset. Service users should be involved in planning, and efforts made to recruit and train disabled staff.

Training

This brings me, last but not least, to the matter of social work training. New social work qualifications are in the process of being introduced and many courses are in the process of revision. This is the time to get it right, therefore. While courses differ widely, some things can probably safely be said about most social work training. Somehow, two years training can seem completely off the point when the student gets a job and starts work. This is partly because many practical issues simply are not dealt with in any systematic way, partly because courses are organised on a piecemeal basis according to lecturers' skills and interests, and partly because it is a long time since many teachers saw the inside of social work office, let alone dealt with a service user. One lecturer, asking for assistance on teaching 'about disability', confessed she had never 'met one of them'. Apart from wondering how she knew that, it is astounding that she should so clearly have thought such a gulf existed.

Unless practical issues are learnt on placement which can be hit and miss, many qualified social workers will emerge never having been inside a DSS office, not having a clue how to apply for an attendance allowance, and having no idea how to manoeuvre a wheelchair up a kerb, let alone dismantle it and get it in the boot. Such things are relatively minor, and easily learnt on the job, but it will not exactly boost confidence when first meeting a parent of a disabled child if you do not know what a 'rollator' (a wheeled walking frame) is for, or what it looks like. Social work trainers who suppose it is acceptable to send students out who do not know their clients' rights under the Education Act, or what the Family Fund provides, are doing disabled children a grave disservice. Practical knowledge is one side of the business, the other is a hard look at attitudes toward disability, and linking the discrimination that children and disabled people face with the oppressions of women, gay people, black racial groups, and so on. Many courses are now tackling this, but the knowledge that disabled children face discrimination is of little help without any idea about their rights.

Social work courses can be as guilty of marginalisation of disabled children as all the other agencies this book has mentioned. Training on disability has traditionally restricted itself to adults, while disability awareness may be no more than a trip to the city centre blindfolded, or in a wheelchair. These somewhat dubious experiences are rendered even more so by their isolation from any structured training programme.

Such treatment separates disabled adults and children from the mainstream. Disability should be part and parcel of all the units on social work courses, from child protection to civil rights. A higher proportion of disabled students on courses would be one way to achieve this raised profile, although that, of course, is another story. It is only by such methods of integration that those with disabilities will emerge as real people, and not remain, as for the lecturer mentioned earlier, 'one of them'.

7. ABUSE

In the Open University text book on 'Child Abuse and Neglect', Geoffrey Watson, in a short chapter on the abuse of disabled children, confesses with great honesty that he had been shocked by his discovery that a disabled child he knew had been sexually abused. 'My own view of social reality had been that handicapped children were sacrosanct, not to be touched. Other children, perhaps, but not the disabled.' (Open University, 1989, p.113.)

Watson's naïve surprise that a disabled child could be abused reflects a common, compartmentalised view that child abuse is one thing, and disability another. Despite this single chapter, disability is scarcely mentioned in the rest of the book. David Jones' *Understanding Child Abuse* a standard social work text on child abuse, ignores the disabled child as victim completely, although it does make reference to a disabled parent as a potential abuser (D.Jones et al. 1987,p.99) and to mental and physical handicap as reasons why people may not be able 'to cope with their lives' (p.282). Failure to take into account the needs for protection of disabled children reflects an insensitivity to their particular vulnerabilities, if nothing else, because of the increased power differential between an abuser and a child who cannot walk, or talk, or hear, or see, or who has limited understanding.

Such neglectful ignorance on the part of child protection workers is not based on a hidden phenomenon, but on a failure to implement in any practical way the findings of research and the dictates of common sense. Social work, it appears, does not WANT to know. As early as 1968, Johnson and Morse reported that 70% of child abuse cases showed some form of developmental problem. (Johnson and Morse, 1968.) Margaret Lynch, a paediatrician, emphasised how a difficult labour and delivery, congenital malformations or injuries at birth, all of which shattered parental hopes for their child, were associated with increased risk of abuse. (Lynch, 1975.) In 1978, the Kempes pointed out that children who are premature, too small or ill, or had defects, or who were stiff and uncuddly, were at risk. Children unable to smile failed to reward their parents. This was not to suggest that physical anomalies caused abuse, but that their existence for some families increased the risk. (Kempe and Kempe, 1978.) In 1982, Goodwin linked physical and mental handicap with vulnerability to sexual abuse. (Goodwin, 1982.) Gegg and Williams, describing child abuse in Liverpool, also cite certain groups of children as being particularly vulnerable: low-weight babies, those separated from their mothers in the early weeks, children with mental or physical handicaps, and children seen by their parents as 'different, strange or overactive' (Gegg and Williams, 1983.) In 1989, Vizard, a child psychiatrist, concluded there are strong pointers in the direction of mental handicap as a risk factor for all forms of child abuse. (Vizard 1989.)

Abuse can be conceptualised as a reaction to stress, and failure of control by parents, or others, to cope with the unremitting demands of a young child, or manage their child's behaviour without recourse to violence. Stressed people feel powerless, and may only regain or retain any sense of control in relation to their even more powerless children. There may be increased pressure where a child is more dependent, less responsive, presents fewer prospects of growing out of its demanding phase, or fails to reward its carers.

The relative helplessness of children with disabilities renders them more likely to be victimised than those who can run, or scream, or tell, or see their tormentor. Disabled children, moreover, who are looked after by a series of people, present wider opportunities for abusers.

Many disabled children are not used to making up their own minds. Children with learning disabilities tend to obey adults, rather than exercise control of their own.

Children who feel themselves unattractive are more likely to feel gratitude for attention. 'Love' may be conditional on acquiescence. In the child's anxiety to be 'normal', sexual abuse is allowed because it means you are 'wanted' and 'all right'.

Social work appears on the one hand to acknowledge that raising disabled children can create stress, but on the other cannot deal with the fact of their being abused by their carers. It brings us back to the stereotypes: the child as sacrosanct; the parent as a saint.

There is a discernible double standard in operation here which results in the same second class service identified in terms of medical care, education and employment. There are a number of reasons why there is a failure to protect.

i. 'It doesn't matter.'

People may believe that there is little point inrrying because these children are damaged already. The abuse somehow matters less. This attitude treats children as chattels, and fails to recqgnise their feelings, let alone their rights. The picture is, however, more complex than the dehumanising of disabled children.

ii. Low value in society.

Jones notes that children are entitled to protection as future citizens. (D. Jones et al, 1987.) Since even disabled adults are frequently not accorded full citizenship, perhaps disabled children too, are not considered as deserving of protection. They are also less likely to grow up and be in a position to take revenge, or abuse the next generation. Disabled children are not always thought to be worth so much. Goodwin tells of a paediatrician who delayed reporting sexual abuse of a young woman with learning difficulties by her three brothers because she thought it better to save three normal boys than one retarded girl. (Goodwin, 1982.)

iii. Failure to connect.

Professional workers tend to go out with a single predetermined purpose to either investigate abuse or to support a family with a disabled child. The belief that work with disabled children is somehow different from child protection means that links, quite simply, are not made. This is the result of categorising children for ease of administration or bureaucratic service delivery. Beyond the failure to make connections there is the failure to consider possibilities. Differences in appearance or behaviour from what seems right are attributed automatically to the disability. Sexuality in disabled children often goes unacknowledged, so that the possibility of sexual abuse is not considered. Walmsley notes that with 'few exceptions unusual behaviour exhibited by children with handicaps tends to be diagnosed and treated from a behaviourist perspective. . . . workers are likely to concentrate on modifying the behaviour without finding its cause'.(Walmsley, 1989.)

iv. Problems in identification.

Identifying abuse can create real problems where a child is disabled, and requires a greater degree of expertise. Yet it is rarely considered necessary to include disabled children as part of the training programmes for child protection workers. Neglect and failure to thrive, with children who do not so readily match centile charts, nor develop according to set programmes, may be harder to detect. Disabled children are often accommodated in segregated residential facilities where care workers are less likely to be trained in child protection. In addition, since the child has been accommodated because of the disability, care staff are unlikely even to consider the possibility of abuse. We are back to the failure to make connections.

The last thing anyone needs is a rash of over-zealous professionals reporting cases of potential abuse because children do not fit their charts of normality. Nevertheless, a disabled child can be neglected very easily, simply by being left unattended, unstimulated or underfed. The story of Anne McDonald, cared for in an Australian hospital for 15 years and emerging at the age of 18 the size of a 5-year-old, graphically illustrates the results of neglect. (Crossley and McDonald, 1980.)

v. Problems in telling.

A disabled child may have even more difficulty reporting abuse than an able-bodied child, because of both a failure to identify what is abuse and communication difficulties.

Disabled children have even less credibility than able-bodied children when reporting abuse. Children with learning disabilities are highly unlikely to be believed in what may be dismissed by adults as a fantastic theory or too much television. The limited credibility is compounded if adults do not recognise the possibility of abuse in the first place. To tell requires a great deal of psychological strength, uncommon in sexually abused children. Not everyone is an enlightened listener.

vi. Limited Options.

There is a lack of options about responses to the abuse of disabled children. Child protection is based on a culture of 'rescue', and social workers need to know what they are rescuing the child *to*. The availability of support in the home, respite and alternative short-term accommodation is very limited, particularly with physically disabled teenagers. Hospital may be the only alternative to an abusing home. There is a pressure for social workers, and others, to ignore something which they feel helpless to do anything about. Child care law is not invoked, and children are left unprotected.

vii. Disablist attitudes.

Put simply, some people want disabled children hidden behind screens and out of sight. They do not want to work with them.

Acknowledgement is needed that, firstly, disabled children are at risk of physical and sexual abuse and, secondly, that they have the same rights to protection as other children are two basic attitudinal steps. Working out how best to help and in what ways special attention may be required are the next stages.

Working with disabled children can present challenges over and above those met with other children if only because the disability needs to be peeled away so that the child can be helped. The social work skills are, however, the same ones: observation, communication, accurate recording and reporting, understanding family dynamics, negotiation, representation, effecting change, and maintaining respect for the civil rights of the individuals concerned.

Communication

Communication with children who have sensory impairments or learning disabilities requires an extended range of skills and techniques, whether in different languages, such as British Sign Language, or by different means, such as play, or by using technological devices, such as light writers. In a multicultural society, not all social workers will be fluent in all languages, which means ensuring there are sufficient fluent social workers for each group, or the use of interpreters.

Speaking a language does not in itself equip a person to be a social worker. For deaf children, Kennedy makes the case for a dual specialist, understanding both abuse and sign language. (Kennedy, 1990a) This is undoubtedly preferable to using an interpreter, but, realistically, dual specialists are thin on the ground, and not all pre-lingually deaf children learn sign language. In the meantime, joint working is essential. (Kennedy, 1990b.)

Children who cannot speak, or use sign language, because of speech or cognitive difficulties, may need to develop alternative methods of communication. There is no recognised alternative language for children with speech problems resulting from conditions such as cerebral palsy, and it is frequently the case that only a close friend or relative is sufficiently tuned in to make sense of distorted speech. One young person with severe disabilities and very slurred speech also has athetoid movements of his arms and legs which grow worse the harder he tries to control them, particularly when he is angry or upset. He has been abused and can only communicate by enlisting the aid of another user at the day centre. While his interpreter is a reliable and caring person, he can, nevertheless, rarely resist sometimes giving his opinions rather than have everyone wait while the disabled young person struggles to voice his own. This flies in the face of most professional and procedural guidelines but such practice is the only way to communicate, and it will need to be accepted that a more flexible approach to people is necessary if all children are to receive protection. If the go between is a member of the family, this can present problems of divided loyalties. The tendency of victims to protect the non-abusing parent from distress is well known, and it is standard practice not to use the mother when investigating sexual abuse.

That attempts to find methods of direct communication have to wait until there is a suspected problem is an indictment of the services currently offered to disabled children. Abused or otherwise, it is important for a child's quality of life that she is helped to acquire communication skills at as high a level as possible, and in whatever form or forms make most sense.

Communication devices for children without speech are at a very basic stage of development and will not solve all the problems. For one thing, neither electronic devices nor symbolics boards are programmed with the sort of vocabulary necessary to discuss abuse, nor to signal messages that might deter abusers. A gigantic step will have been made in equal opportunities when a Bliss board first gets a 'PISS OFF' symbol.

Communicating with a child in distress who has no speech is a time-consuming and difficult task. It is not the same as communicating with a very young child, and it is important not to assume poor speech means poor understanding. It is important also to keep the child calm, and make it clear you have as long as it takes, either by saying so, or by demonstrating it by taking off your coat, and sitting down. Social workers who visit people and keep their coats on and perch on the edge of their seats demonstrate to the individual only that they have more pressing engagements. Calming someone who has athetoid movements, like the young man described, will help minimise them. The same goes for less serious problems like a stutter. Once the child is settled, establishing a clear YES/NO signal is the next step. Most children will already have one, so simply asking them to show you how they say YES and how they say NO may suffice. Most things can be communicated, given patience and practice in asking the right questions, using a YES/NO signal. It is, of course, the very opposite of the open-ended questioning technique usually recommended in order not to lead, and is only suggested if there is no other option. It is a tiring process, and can be very frustrating for the disabled person if the interviewer persists in asking the wrong questions.

Touch and Privacy

Disabled children may have different views of the world because of their different experience of upbringing. This can cause confusion about cause and effect that is even more marked than that in able-bodied children. Kennedy points out that a deaf child who has learned that deaf is a 'bad thing' may conclude that they have been abused because they are deaf. (Kennedy 1990a). This 'conclusion' may well be true, given the greater chance of the abuse going undetected and the lesser respect shown to disabled children, but not for the reason the child supposes: i.e. as a punishment. Disabled young people who require intimate physical care may develop different views on the meaning of touch from able bodied adolescents. Touch is associated with personal hygiene, cleaning up and toileting rather than with affection or cuddling. Some institutionalised children may only be touched when they are dirty: a deeply dehumanising socialisation process. It is important that children experience affectionate touching, so that they can distinguish what is not. Basic rules of thumb such as teaching children that intimate touching by adults need never be a secret thing can be more difficult to apply with young people who have a right to personal care in private. It is doubly important, therefore, that such children are not kept ignorant of sex nor uninformed about the meaning of the changes in their bodies or the feelings they are experiencing.

Safety programmes have been developed largely for use in schools, over the last ten years or so, based on the premise that children can be taught to avoid the dangers of abuse in the same way they can be taught about fire or road safety. Teaching children about abuse is controversial, based on beliefs about the sanctity of childhood, meaning that children should not be burdened with responsibilities too early in life. If this protection from responsibility is at the expense of the child's safety the argument looks shaky. However, there are real dangers that expecting children to avoid abuse themselves places greater pressure on those who have not told or have not run. It also shifts the responsibility for prevention onto the child and away from the adults, whose duty it properly is. Recognising the vulnerability of children to abuse should not be confused with assuming it is the fault of the victim.

Society operates according to the wishes and desires of the adult population. In many respects the abuse of children by some is taken as an acceptable risk by all in return for the continuation of family privacy and parental power. Some shift in attitude is required that is based on valuing children, seeking to protect them from pain and acknowledging they have rights. If this appears a gigantic step where able-bodied children are concerned it must appear an even greater hurdle where the child is disabled and even less valued by society. While society fails to take seriously the issue of disabled children who are abused the message to perpetrators remains that, even if not all right, it is certainly not as grave as assaulting or neglecting a non-disabled child. A parent caring for a disabled child is already seen by society as carrying a heavier burden, and therefore there is more ready tolerance of their abusing.

Responding to Abuse

Should education of children and protection by adults fail, and children suffer abuse, it is at least important to recognise its existence, and take it seriously. This involves not only responding to the immediate situation, but dealing with the long term consequences for the children who have been victimised. If abuse is suspected, the social worker, and probably the police, will have to investigate. The enquiry into alleged abuse is not simply to seek to establish whether or not an application to court is necessary, but whether the local authority should be providing services. Schedule 2, Section 4, of the Children Act places a duty on local authorities to act to prevent harm, ill treatment or neglect. Preventive services are not bound, as in the past, by the criteria of forestalling an admission to care, but are much broader. During what may be a very difficult period for the family, it is important that the social worker keeps in mind the primary responsibility to the child, whether or not the suspicions prove groundless, not proven, or substantiated. BASW refers to this in their guidelines on managing child sexual abuse as a child-centred philosophy. (BASW, 1990.) This may not be as easy as it sounds given society's ambivalent attitude towards child protection, which both expects social workers to carry the burden of protecting children as well as respecting the family's right to privacy. BASW's guidelines are appropriate to all forms of abuse, and apply to all children, although some extra care will be required with some disabled children. It is recommended that the length of interviews is kept to a minimum, even if this means a series of sessions, and take place in surroundings where the child feels comfortable. This is not necessarily the home, if the abuse occurred there. They should be at the child's pace. If there are communication problems, however, the interview may proceed at the speed at which the social worker is able to understand. It is important not to lead the child, given that the interview may later be needed as evidence. Using a video recorder saves the child having to repeat themselves over and over again, but they require operating and setting up, and this may not always be practicable. BASW stresses that children rarely lie about sexual abuse and, unlike physical abuse, there may be no physical signs. It is important to start from a point of accepting the child's story.

If access to a child is refused the local authority can make an application to the court for a child assessment order (CAO), or, if the situation is more serious, an emergency protection order. The application for a CAO will be heard by the full court, and all parties may be represented. The CAO requires those caring for a child to produce her. If granted it will last for seven days, which will probably be used for a medical examination, for which the child's consent is required. In more urgent circumstances, a single magistrate can grant an emergency protection order if it is considered that the child would otherwise suffer significant harm. This would enable the local authority to retain the child in safe accommodation, or remove them to it. It does not allow them to ban parents unless the court specifically directs. An alternative to the above is that the police can take the child into their protection for up to 72 hours if they have reasonable cause to believe the child would otherwise suffer significant harm. Action, following, or at the same time as, the investigation, takes a number of lines. These may include actions to protect, care proceedings in the civil court, and a prosecution in the criminal court.

Action to Protect

Since abuse is an abuse of power, the social worker should take whatever steps are available to give the child more power. This means alerting, and supporting, potential allies such as relatives or teachers, as well as non-abusing parents or carers. It may mean involving the police if the abuse is serious. Clearly, the latter decision is based on professional experience and consultation with senior colleagues. It may involve a decision to separate the child from the alleged abuser. Both BASW and the Children's Legal Centre recommend it is the alleged abuser who is removed. (BASW 1990; CHILDRIGHT Jan/Feb 1990.)

The Children Act clearly replaces the notion of parental rights with one of parental responsibility. If an abusing parent will not voluntarily leave the home, the Children's Legal Centre recommends the welfare principle of the Act is invoked and an ouster order made to exclude the alleged perpetrator from the home. Even if the adult is wrongly excluded he has more chance of understanding the reasons for it than the child. This principle applies equally in a residential setting, and should be easier to effect since the employer has the power to exclude.

Should the alleged abuser refuse to leave, and there be insufficient evidence to compel him, a family may still agree to a separation but only if it is the child who leaves. In this case, or, indeed, simply where a family believe they need such help, the local authority can provide accommodation. This is on an agreed basis with the parents who can ask for the child back at any time. This replaces the old concept of 'voluntary care', which was often not voluntary at all, with one where the local authority should be seen to be offering a service. This is to 'look after' a child where the carers are prevented from caring, either temporarily or permanently, for whatever reason. Such a decision is never easy, but the way in which it is presented can make all the difference. Care meant that parents had failed. Having a child 'looked after' emphasises that raising a child is the responsibility of the whole society. The distinction may help the parents more than the child, however, increasing the need for the social worker to try to retain the child's sense of worth, rather than allow her to believe she is nothing more than a burden. This is not an easy task, partly because, for her family, she *is* seen as a burden. A major problem with this approach is the dearth of suitable short term accommodation for disabled children, particularly physically disabled teenagers. Children still wait in hospitals for appropriate placements which are often planned by the agencies that provide them as long term.

Care Proceedings

Should care proceedings be thought necessary, an application for a care or supervision order can be made through the courts. If there is clear evidence of physical abuse, the local authority will have to prove that it can make a better job of caring. A care order can only be made if the court is satisfied that doing so would be better for the child than making no order at all. The court must therefore consider the local authority's plans for the child. Given the above noted shortage of suitable accommodation, this may not prove very easy. The criteria for care or supervision that the child concerned has suffered significant harm, or is likely to do so, and that the harm is attributable to the parents not giving reasonable care, or the child being beyond their control. (S31(2).) Children with challenging behaviour will fall into the last-mentioned group. The child must be shown to be suffering or likely to suffer a substantial deficit in the standard of health or development which it is reasonable to expect her to achieve. (Review of Child Care Law, para. 15.14.)

Clearly, there are going to be problems with the latter recommendation, since the expectations of health and development for disabled children are different from able-bodied children. It may prove impossible to separate what is the fault of neglectful parents and what is attributable to disability or chronic ill health.

Disabled children may have to suffer very substantial neglect before it is possible to act. In neither case, however, is it necessary to prove WHO committed the abuse in order to take steps to protect the child either by removal or by enforcing supervision.

Criminal Proceedings

If there are contested criminal proceedings a child may be an essential witness. Sexual abuse, as with able-bodied children, is notoriously hard to prove if denied by the alleged abuser, and the testimony of the child may be crucial. The decision as to whether to use a child witness rests with the Director of Public Prosecutions, relying on the advice of the police. It is not the decision of the child. The police obviously, are protective of children, and may prove especially so if the child has a disability. Nevertheless, some children may resent not being consulted.

Court can be stressful. The Children's Legal Centre makes a number of suggestions on easing this (CLC, Jan/Feb 1990), and also issue an advice sheet written for children of eight and above, although they advise it is used with the support of an adult. (CLC, March 1990.) Clearly, the age at which a child with learning disabilities will understand will vary. Courts, deliberately designed to awe, are not very user friendly. Old men with long white wigs, wearing their dressing gowns in the day-time, are enough to make *anyone* forget their name and address!

Thankfully, courts are increasingly dispensing with these antiquated costumes when a child is involved.

There is no reason why the child cannot rehearse being in court, and she certainly needs firm advice about what is all right and what is not. It is, for example, all right to say 'I don't know', or 'I don't understand the question', to ask for a drink, or to go to the toilet. Visiting court beforehand is one means of demystifying it. Children over 14 can visit a court in session, while those younger than that can at least be taken to see the court,have it explained to them. It may be possible to get barristers to relax their usual code and meet the child witness beforehand. If both defending and prosecuting barristers are present this prevents accusations of coaching. The Court Listing Officer may, if notified early enough, be able to arrange for the least intimidating court to be used. It may help if a microphone is provided to prevent a frightened child having to 'speak up'.

A video link is now allowed in the court in child abuse cases where the child is under 14. Some prior experience of being taped may therefore be helpful. It is also possible to use pre-recorded interviews for statements, although cross-questioning will still be live, whether direct, screened or by video link.

There has been some discussion about the use of supporters for child witnesses. The problem is the fear that the supporter will give the child the answers. A victim supporter at one Crown Court, passing a distressed child's handkerchief, was instructed to do so 'palm upwards'.

With disabled children, some of these patterns need to be challenged. A supporter would be essential for a severely disabled child without speech, or a visually impaired child unable to see what was going on. In addition, speakers may need to identify themselves and not assume the child can recognise voices. Children therefore need a great deal of preparation before a court appearance, not to get their story straight, but to make sure the stresses and strangeness of the day do not confuse and intimidate them into silence. Disabled children, above all others, are conditioned to be neither seen nor heard. They are used to people speaking for them, a pattern which can continue into adulthood, and suddenly being asked to answer questions may prove far too much to handle. In practice, therefore, many disabled children will be unable to attend court as witnesses, and prosecutions will not be made.

Victim Support

Failure to secure a prosecution in no way reduces responsibilities to victims. Long-term support will be required no less than for non-disabled children. Long-term support and therapeutic counselling for victims and families are not easy work. It needs commitment, the ability to deal with complex emotions and the willingness not to judge. In particular, where sexual abuse has occurred, some very difficult concepts have to be taken on board by the worker before any open minded, realistic counselling can start:

* many paedophiles are very good with children, and are liked by them.

* some children may have enjoyed the attention and the sexual contact.

Workers in this field have to work out their own feelings not only about abuse and what is acceptable to them, but also about disability. Difficulties in communication with some children are sometimes used as an excuse not to provide help. If a child picks up feelings of dislike or revulsion, they are likely to blame themselves and the fact of their disability. This will reinforce their poor self image. Counselling has to start from a position of accepting the child, and acknowledging how they are feeling: even if this contrasts sharply with how the worker feels; how the worker felt if they were abused or how the worker thinks the child should feel. The child may well not hate the abuser, nor blame them, and in fact express feelings of affection for them. Some acknowledgement that the abuser may not be all bad is a necessary meeting place with a victim who feels this way, before any progress on relocating blame or restoring self worth can be made. Counselling abused children involves dealing with the question of their being 'bad'. Where the child is disabled this badness is often put onto the disability, becoming 'I was abused because I am different/not strong/a disappointment to my parents'. Counselling therefore involves exploring not only the abuse but also how the child feels about their disability; their body; themself. A range of methods are available,depending on the age of the child, such as play-acting, drawing, using dolls or picture books.

Abused children blame themselves, especially if they did not try to stop the abuse, and the counselling process has to work toward telling children of their powerlessness in relation to an adult abuser. This blame may be shared by the non-abusing parent, usually the mother. She may feel guilty, both for not protecting her child and because the child was unable to tell her. The child may grow angry at not being protected. If the abuser is thrown out, the mother may expect gratitude, which is rarely forthcoming. The worker faces an angry child and a guilty mother. This can be compounded for a disabled child who may conclude she has not been protected because the disability makes her parents think her less worthy of it. That this may be true does not make untangling the family dynamics any easier. Such feelings have to be acknowledged before they can be redirected to move the responsibility where it rightly belongs: on to the abuser. Men have proved experts at putting the whole blame for abuse onto women and children, and this is a situation that should not be acquiesced in by the worker. An abused child may also experience longer term problems about their sexuality. A male child abused by a man is going to question whether this makes him a homosexual. A child who experiences sexual intercourse at an early age will find it hard to identify with school friends giggling behind the bike shed at their first kiss. Sexuality for disabled children is even more confused given the possibility of denial of adequate sex education. Not all these issues are likely to crop up at once, but can occur years after the abuse is discovered.

Both supportive and therapeutic groups have proved valuable means of helping survivors of sexual abuse and, while there is no reason why these should not include disabled children, the complications of the disability might indicate the need for groups of disabled or deaf survivors. There can be difficulties in organising such groups both on a practical level and because of the smaller known 'pool' of survivors on which to draw. Nevertheless, many survivors will at least appreciate the opportunity to be put in touch with each other, even if therapeutic groups are few and far between. On the other hand, a group of survivors both disabled and non-disabled may aid the disabled person separate their abuse from their disability, by appreciating that able-bodied children are also abused. This may help reduce negative feelings about the disability.

Social work therefore aims to provide means of helping victims repair the damage and rebuild personalities. This involves accepting the individual, and their experience, and helping them to feel positive about themselves. It is a relatively new area of social work, and no one has any blue-prints, making it particularly important that experiences and ideas are shared.

8. MOVING ON

This book started by reflecting on the images and roles of disabled people. It went on to discuss the ways in which disability is nurtured both by society and by families, so that a child with an impairment is marginalised by society. I discussed this in terms of a series of hurdles to be overcome before a person could fully participate as an equal member of society. However, we should be wary that in discarding the medical model of an individual struggling to overcome disability to gain acceptance by becoming as near able-bodied as possible, we do not invent another model in which an individual is left to struggle alone for equality in an oppressive society, perhaps by seeking to become an exception to the general rule about disabled people. Although it must often seem so to disabled people and their supporters, the fight for equal opportunities should not be an individual struggle, but part of a much wider one concerning the civil rights of all members of society. In this sense it extends beyond the bounds of the disability movement, and connects with other equal opportunity issues such as oppression by reason of race, gender or age. Nevertheless, while members of these groups can seek to make their own voices heard, children's safety and quality of life are clearly the responsibility of adults. For social workers this means establishing partnerships with parents and carers, not only to meet their immediate and individual needs, but to help them to look beyond to the struggle for equality for their children.

This means teaching the child to value and respect themself and others, based on the belief that they have as much right to be there as anyone else. It follows that the picture of a disabled child as an object of charity and pity has to be repainted.

Children have to be involved, without denying their rights to be children. The profile of disabled children on the agendas of those agencies, statutory and voluntary, where they are currently marginalised will have to be raised. Good practice does exist, and should be identified, publicised and built on. It is for workers in this field to ask questions, make connections, demystify, educate and make continuing challenge to oppressive attitudes, language and practices.

One forum for addressing some of these issues is conferences. These can be expensive, and may deny service users access because of this alone, so planning with users in mind does matter. Smaller local workshops may be cheaper and more accessible. There is not any magic formula for these, as different things work for different people. However, I would suggest there is a core agenda:

1.— ATTITUDES towards disability have to be explored, and done so without intimidation. All of us have continually to untangle the socialisations of our childhoods, as well as the continuing influences around us every day.

2.— KNOWLEDGE has to be acquired, and shared. Knowledge is power and brings the means to change things. It widens horizons by revealing possibilities.

3.— SKILLS, such as communicating, have to be acquired and practised.

4.— CONFIDENCE has to be developed, and then put to use.

The development of effective ways of working with disabled children and their carers is a dynamic process. Workshops are about people sharing ideas and exploring those of others. I hesitate therefore to be prescriptive, and offer the following only as one or two ideas to get things moving.

The Child's Eyes

This exercise involves a small group of adults making a conscious effort to see things from the point of view of a child. (It is expressly NOT a role play, nor an attempt to pretend to be or act like a child.) Some knowledge of child development helps, and the fixing of an age, before the group sets itself the task of identifying what would be important to the child, and what they would want. The workshop leader should sketch-in details of a real or imaginary family or care situation, without unnecessary confusing detail, and let the group think its way into someone else's shoes. This is never easy, but in practice we find it easier to empathise with adult carers needs because we are adults, and this kind of exercise can help retune our thinking.

Translated into the real world, this should have two benefits. It raises the profile of the child's perspective so that the worker is more likely to consider it and it eases communication with the child because their *possible* hopes and fears have already been through the worker's mind. It should be stressed that neither this, nor the next exercise is intended to be a substitute for listening, in the real world, to what children actually communicate.

A Day at the Nursery

Also from the perspective of a child, run through a day in a nursery. If there are disabled adults in the group, charge them with emphasising any barriers the nursery's structure or regime may create for a child with a similar disability. Best done in a nursery. Try looking at life from the floor.

Looking Back

It is an education to adults who grew up without disabilities to listen to those who faced extra difficulties in childhood.

Try putting yourself in these shoes, for example :

'I can remember as a small child going to PE with my pump bag containing one pump. My left leg was in a calliper and surgical boot. I no longer go swimming or anything, but really that is just vanity.'

A 20-year-old, writing about himself. (Private communication.)

Life History

As an awareness-raising exercise, compare the probable life history of a child abandoned at birth who is able-bodied with a child who has severe disabilities. A generation ago this would have been a stark difference between adoption on the one hand and life in hospital on the other. What are the possibilities today?

Respite

Respite is a term used for relief from the pressure of caring for a disabled child. Yet all carers need breaks from their children. Explore ways in which carers of able-bodied children get their respite, and ask some questions about why these avenues cannot be opened to all.

Counselling

It helps if groups consider ways of helping, by sharing experience and ideas in a supportive way. The formula is to minimise confusing detail, and maximise the opportunity for the group to discuss the issues. The following is one possibility:

The idea that disabled children are born to bad parents perhaps has little currency nowadays but there remains,nevertheless, a stigma attached to the birth of a child who is not 'all right'.

Charlie, a gunner based in a barracks near Preston, found he could not face his mates any more after his son was born with cerebral palsy.

At the moment, Charlie sees it all as his problem, but there are at least three people to help in this situation : Charlie, his wife,and his son.

What are the implications for the son if nothing changes in Charlie's thinking?

Telling the News

Much attention is given to how parents are told about their child's disability. Sometimes the shock caused by the way they are told is, in itself, a major problem.

Looking at it from the child's angle:

How should your parents learn about your disability?

Participation

Devise a means of enabling disabled children to attend their own case reviews *without being an unequal participant.*

Stories

Try telling stories in which disabled children are the stars. . . and NOT for 'overcoming' their disability! In this age of flip charts, you could even try sketching a cartoon or writing a film script.

The more of these stories are true, of course, the better it is for everyone!

Engaging in these, and similar, exercises with others committed to improving life for disabled children, should help refine attitudes and improve self-confidence, to enable workers to tackle the barriers and prejudices of the real world. There is much to be done.

REFERENCES

Advisory Centre on Education (1983) *ACE Special Handbook.*

Anderson, E. and Spain, B. (1977) *The Child with Spina Bifida.* Methuen.

Baldwin, S. (1985) *The Cost of Caring.* RKP.

Barclay Report (1982) *Social Workers: Their Roles and Tasks*
NISW/Bedford Square Press.

Barnes, C. (1989) *The Cabbage Syndrome.* Falmer.

BASW (1990) *Management of Child Sexual Abuse.* BASW Report.

Battye (1966) The Chatterley Syndrome. In Hunt, P. (ed) *Stigma - the
Experience of Disability.* Chapman.

Billinsley, A. and Giovanni, J. (1972) *Children of the Storm: Black
Children and American Child Welfare.* Harcourt Brace Jovanovich Inc.

Bodegard, G. Fyro, K. and Larsson, A. (1983) Psychological reactions in
102 families with a newborn who has a false positive screening test for
congenital hypothyroidism. *Acta Paediatrica Scandinavica Supplement
304* (Quoted in Lindsay G. 1984)

Brown, C. (1954) *My Left Foot.* Martin Secker and Warburg.

Brown, H. and Craft, A. (1989) *Thinking the Unthinkable.* FPA
Education Unit.

Burton, L. (1975) *The Family Life of Sick Children.* London RKP.

CCETSW (1974) Paper 5. *People with handicaps need better trained workers.*

Chartered Society of Phsyiotherapy (1975) *Handling the Handicapped.* Woodhead-Faulkner.

Children's Legal Centre (Jan/Feb. 1990) *The Child Witness.* Information sheet.

Children's Legal Centre (March 1990) *Being a Witness.* Information sheet.

Childright News Team (Jan/Feb 1990) *Remove alleged abusers, not children.* Childright.

Crossley, R. and MacDonald, A. (1980) *Annie's Coming Out.* Penguin.

CSIE (1983) *Kirsty: the struggle for a place in an ordinary school.* CSIE Factsheet.

Curtis Report (1946) *Report of the Care of Children Committee.* Cmd 6922 HMSO.

Dept. of Educ. (1989) *Employment and Training of People with Disabilities.*

Dept. of Health (1988) *Implementing the Disabled Persons (Services, Consultation and Representation) Act 1986.* S.S.I.

Duffy, M. (1990) Yes, I do take sugar when I get a chance. In *Observer 2.9.90.*

Finch, J. and Groves, D. (1983) *A Labour of Love: Women, Work and Caring.* RKP.

Finnie, N. (1974) *Handling the Young Cerebral Palsied Child at Home.* Weinemann.

Freeman, R.D. Carbin, C.F. and Boese, R.J. (1981) *Can't Your Child Hear?* Croom Helm.

Fry, E. (1987) *Disabled People and the 1987 General Election.* Spastics Society.

Furneaux (1988) *Special Parents.* OUP

Gegg, A.J. and Williams, J.K. (1983) Child Abuse Treatment in Liverpool, England. In Ebeling, N.B. and Hill, D.A. *Child Abuse and Neglect.* John Wright.

GLAD (1990) *Speaking for Ourselves.* Greater London Association for Disabled People.

Glendinning, C. (1983) *Unshared Care: Parents and their Disabled Children.* RKP.

Glendinning, C. (1986) *A Single Door: Social Work With the Families of Disabled Children.* Allen and Unwin.

Goodwin, J. (1982) *Sexual Abuse: Incest Victims and their Families.* John Wright.

Halliday, P. (1989) *Children with Physical Disability.* Cassell.

Hannam, C. (1989) *Parents and Mentally Handicapped Children.* Penguin (2nd Ed).

Harris, Louis and Associates (1975) Myths and Realities of Life for Older Americans (The Harris Poll). In *Perspectives on Ageing.* March/April 1975.

House of Commons Select Committee (1987) Third Report from the Education and Science and Arts Committee. *Special Education Needs: Implementation of the Education Act 1981.* HMSO.

Johnson, B. and Morse, H.A. (1968) Injured Children and their Parents. In *Children*. 1968, 15.

Jones, D.N., Pickett, J., Oates, M.R. and Barbor (1987) *Understanding Child Abuse*. Macmillan (2nd Ed).

Jones, G. (1989) Women in Social Care. In C. Hallett (ed) *Women in Social Services Departments*. p.144.

Kempe, R.S. and Kempe, C.H. (1978) *Child Abuse*. Open Books.

Kennedy, M. (1990a) The Deaf Child Who is Sexually Abused. In *Child Abuse Review*. number 2.

Kennedy, M. (1990b) Overcoming Myths: The Abused Disabled Child. In *Concern*. Summer 1990.

Lane, S. (1990) *Report to Liverpool Early Years Centre Development Project*. (Personal Communication).

Lansdown, R. (1980) *More than Sympathy: The Everyday Needs of Sick and Handicapped Children and their Families*. Tavistock.

Lindsay, G. (ed) (1984) *Screening for Children with Special Needs*. Croom Helm.

Linehan, T. (1990) Freeing Alter Egos. In *Care Weekly* 24.8.90.

Local Government Training Board (1990) *The Disabling Council*. (Video).

Lynch, M.A. (1975) Ill Health and Child Abuse, *Lancet 2*. p.317.

Morgan (1975) Social Aspects of Integration. In Loring, J. and Burn, G. *Integration of Handicapped Children in Society*. RKP and the Spastics Society.

O'Brien, J. and Lyle, C. (1987) *Frame for Accomplishment*. Georgie Responsive Systems Associates.

O'Grady, C. (1990) *Integration Working*. CSIE Report.

Oliver, M. (1983) *Social Work with Disabled People*. Macmillan.

Oliver, M. (1990) *The Politics of Disablement*. Macmillan.

Oliver, M. (1990) Handicapped by the Wrong Word. in *Observer. 2.9.90*.

OPCS (1986) *Survey of Disability in Great Britain*. HMSO.

Open University (1990) *Disability - Changing Practice*. (Video.)

Oswin, M. (1984) *They keep going away*. KingsFund/OUP.

Robinson, B. (1987) Key issues for social workers placing children for family based respite care. In *British Journal of Social Work 17*.

Robson, B. (1989) *Pre-School Provision for Children with Special Needs*. Cassell.

Sefton Social Services (1990) *Report to BASW Conference*.

Shaw, L. (1990) *Each Belongs: Integrated Education in Canada*. CSIE Report.

Shearer, A. (1981) *Disability: Whose Handicap?* Basil Blackwell.

Spain, B. and Wigley, G. (ed) (1975) *Right from the Start*. NSMHC.

Stalker, K. (1987) *Share the Care: A Research Report of Lothians Respite Scheme for Children with Handicaps*. Lothian Regional Council.

Sutherland, A. (1981) *Disabled We Stand*. Souvenir Press.

Vizard, E. (1989) Child Sexual Abuse and Mental Handicap: A child psychiatrist's perspective. In Brown and Craft *Thinking the Unthinkable*. FPA.

Voysey, M. (1975) *A Constant Burden*. RKP.

Wakefield, T. (1978) *Some Mothers I Know*. RKP.

Walmsley, S. (1989) The need for safeguards. In Brown and Craft *Thinking the Unthinkable*. RKP.

Watson, G. (1989) The Abuse of Disabled Children and Young People. In Rogers, W.S., Hevey, D. and Ash, E. (ed) *Child Abuse and Neglect*. Batsford/Open University.

White, R., Carr, P. and Lowe, N. (1990) *A Guide to the Children Act 1989*. Butterworths.

USEFUL ADDRESSES

Children's Legal Centre
 20 Compton Terrace
London
N1 2UN
071 359 6251

Child Abuse Project
National Deaf Children's Society
Nuffield Hearing & Speech Centre
325 Gray's Inn Road
London, WC1X ODA
071 833 5627

CSIE
4th Floor
4/5 Edgware Road
London
NW2 6NB
081 452 8642

Family Fund
P.O Box 50
York
YO1 2ZX

Young Carers Project
Carers National Association
29 Chilworth Mews
London, W2 3RG
071 724 7776